"Most Christians would tell you they believe the Bible to be God's Word. And yet many of those same Christians could not even articulate what the core beliefs are to the Christian faith. In *Jesus Loves Me*, John Dickerson does a great job of helping believers understand the basic teachings of Scripture. This is a great resource for any Christian who needs to build a stronger foundation to their faith."

Steve Poe, lead pastor of Northview Church, Carmel, Indiana

Praise for *Jesus Skeptic*

"*Jesus Skeptic* is a different kind of book. It examines the positive social impact of those who believe in Jesus. That impact is widespread and far greater than most people realize. Moving from one area to another, Dickerson documents that influence and then looks deeper into what and who is behind it. This is a fascinating read that may just surprise you."

Dr. Darrell L. Bock, *New York Times* bestselling author and senior research professor of New Testament studies at Dallas Theological Seminary

"My hometown of Portland, Oregon, is filled with wonderful people, especially millennials, who gravely misunderstand who Jesus ~ have little understanding of the ways his foll~ city and the world a better place. written a much-needed book to he church, of the community of peop more than two thousand years, is a that has shaped education and heal ~cientific inquiry, helped to abolish slavery, and le~ ~.ie way in protecting human rights. Understanding this impact can encourage wavering believers and soften the hearts of many skeptics."

Kevin Palau, president of the Luis Palau Association

"As with his other work, Dickerson's words are extremely insightful and relevant."

Dr. Jim Denison, CEO of Denison Forum and author of *How Does God See America?*

"This generation isn't simply asking, 'Is Christianity true?' They want to know, 'Is Christianity *good*? Does the faith actually promote human rights, alleviate suffering, and enable humanity to flourish?' In *Jesus Skeptic*, John Dickerson provides a compelling answer to these pressing questions. He leads readers on a lively tour through the ancient world, demonstrating Christianity's positive impact at key moments in history. This book is a remarkable accomplishment.

It is sweeping in scope yet deeply personal. Dickerson, a reporter and pastor, reveals Christianity's impact on history—then zooms in to explore what Christ means for each person. The evidence Dickerson offers will enlighten believers and non-believers alike. In the introduction, he writes that skeptics 'are safe here.' That's true—but their skepticism is definitely in danger."

Drew Dyck, contributing editor at CTPastors.com and author of *Your Future Self Will Thank You*

"Only John Dickerson could so artfully weave history, politics, pop culture, and personal stories in a way that is both educational and entertaining. As a devout agnostic, I thoroughly enjoyed learning about a different perspective—presented in a thoughtful, engaging, and enlightening way."

Amy Silverman, award-winning journalist, editor, and author of *My Heart Can't Even Believe It*

"Many scholarly works make points and arguments for Christ and Christianity similar to those John Dickerson makes here; however, his book seems more readable and engaging than most. The length seems ideal for the book's intended audience—not so short as to appear inconsequential, yet not so lengthy as to be uninviting. It is well worth reading!"

Dr. Hugh Ross, astronomer, pastor, and president of Reasons to Believe

"My good friend John S. Dickerson has unearthed his biggest story ever as an investigative reporter. *Jesus Skeptic* is an eye-opening and desperately needed resource in a world of revisionist history. Honest skeptics as well as parents and pastors will find facts—not opinions—to answer their most challenging questions about Jesus's life, teaching, and impact in history. I highly recommend this book."

Chip Ingram, author of *Why I Believe* and teaching pastor at Living on the Edge

"More than ever we need an articulate and detailed study of the importance and impact of the Christian faith that is not charged with emotions but is loaded with evidence. I am pleased to recommend John's work to you, knowing that it will surprise you and draw you into the greater narrative of God's unfolding mission within history. If you are a skeptic, this book is especially for you, and John's arguments and research will intrigue you and invite you further into dialogue with history's most significant person, Jesus."

Ed Stetzer, executive director of the Billy Graham Center

JESUS

LOVES

[ME]

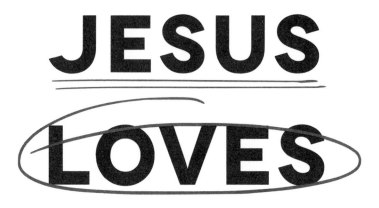

JESUS LOVES {ME}

CHRISTIAN ESSENTIALS FOR
THE HEAD AND THE HEART

JOHN S. DICKERSON

BakerBooks

a division of Baker Publishing Group
Grand Rapids, Michigan

© 2021 by John S. Dickerson

Published by Baker Books
a division of Baker Publishing Group
PO Box 6287, Grand Rapids, MI 49516-6287
www.bakerbooks.com

Printed in the United States of America

Library of Congress Cataloging-in-Publication Data
Names: Dickerson, John S., author.
Title: Jesus loves me : Christian essentials for the head and the heart / John S.
    Dickerson.
Description: Grand Rapids, Michigan : Baker Books, a division of Baker Publishing
    Group, 2021. | Includes bibliographical references.
Identifiers: LCCN 2020019700 | ISBN 9780801078095 (paperback) | ISBN
    9781540901491 (casebound)
Subjects: LCSH: Christianity—Essence, genius, nature. | Jesus loves me.
Classification: LCC BT60 .D53 2021 | DDC 230—dc23
LC record available at https://lccn.loc.gov/2020019700

Published in association with Ambassador Literary Agency, Nashville, Tennessee.

21 22 23 24 25 26 27   7 6 5 4 3 2 1

If you hold to my teaching,
you are really my disciples.
Then you will know the truth,
and the truth will set you free.

John 8:31–32

Contents

WHY SHOULD YOU READ THIS BOOK?

If I want to experience God's power and salvation, what do I need to believe? If I respect Jesus, does it really matter what I believe?

This book answers these questions and helps you know what you believe as a follower of Jesus. It's a primer on basic Christian beliefs. Read it to completion, and you will know how to access the power of God. You will learn the essentials any person or church must hold in order to experience Jesus on His terms.

Let's begin by answering this question: *Do the basic beliefs really matter?*

Yes.

These essential beliefs are a matter of life and death.

Here's a fascinating true story that demonstrates why you must know what you believe.

My friend Ralph serves as a fire chief in Arizona. One day Ralph was driving in his pickup when he heard an emergency call on his firefighter radio. The 911 operator was sending out a distress call; an infant had stopped breathing.

A baby had been left in a hot car at a gas station. The Arizona sun had baked the parked car, raising its interior temperature to 120+ degrees. By the time the child's mom realized she had left her baby in the car, the little girl was unresponsive, moments away from death.

Ralph listened, waiting to hear the address of the gas station where the accident occurred. When the street name was given, Ralph realized he was only two blocks away. He could get to this dying child faster than any fire crew in town.

He hit the brakes, did a quick U-turn, floored the accelerator, and sped toward the gas station where a terrified young mom was cradling her lifeless infant.

When Ralph got to the scene, he jumped out of his truck. With the speed of a trained professional, he scooped the baby away from the mom, who was screaming and crying uncontrollably.

Ralph knew exactly what to do. He shouted for people to go inside and get ice to cool the baby's body temperature, then immediately began CPR on the tiny infant who was cradled in his two hands.

If you ever take a CPR class, you will learn that CPR rescue breaths, also known as mouth-to-mouth resuscitation, work differently with a small child. On an adult, you plug the person's nose with your hand and place your mouth over their mouth. On a small child, though, you put your mouth over the child's entire nose and mouth together. This way the rescue breaths can quickly fill the tiny lungs.

As Ralph breathed into the lifeless child's mouth and nose, he watched as his own breath entered her lungs. He could see the baby's chest rise up, now filled with the breath from his own lungs.

After giving the right number of breaths, Ralph started to give the accompanying small pushes on the chest to restart that baby's tiny heart.

You've likely seen how doctors or paramedics on TV push down on an adult's chest during CPR, with full-force compressions, using both hands and straight arms. It's different with a little baby. Because the heart is so small and the body so fragile, you just use two fingers to firmly press into the sternum, or chest bone, to restart the unmoving heart. An infant's heart is so little and beats so fast that these rapid, miniature compressions work best.

Ralph was giving those rapid compressions with his two fingers on the baby's chest. He was breathing those short breaths into those tiny lungs, and all along Ralph was wondering, *Is this little girl going to live or not? Did I get here fast enough?* As a believer in Jesus, Ralph was praying for God's help and intervention, even while he did everything in his own power to resuscitate the child.

Ralph then experienced the most unbelievable moment—an incredible sensation few others have experienced. He had his mouth on this baby's face, and he was praying, timing his breathing, and doing everything he could to save the infant's life.

Then—after he exhaled once again—Ralph felt the baby breathe back out.

What a moment. The baby began gasping and crying, breathing and living. Her heart, not moving just moments ago, began beating. The little girl opened her eyes.

Ralph continued holding the baby, monitoring her and calming her down as much as possible. He continued to watch closely. That day, he breathed life back into a baby who was otherwise dead.

It's an incredible true story. And it's a picture of what God did when He came to earth. You see, God's Word describes that, before we believe in Jesus, we are spiritually dead in our mistakes and sins. God came into this earth to breathe life into us. Just like Ralph raced to that gas station to save that infant, God raced into our world, in the person of Jesus, to save us.

This is why Jesus declared: "I have come that they may have life, and have it to the full" (John 10:10).

Jesus came to breathe life into our souls. He came to breathe eternal life into us, so that we can be with God in heaven after we leave this earth.

He came to breathe this life into all who will believe and receive His free gift of salvation.

Wherever we are dead in our wrongdoings, Jesus races into our world to breathe life back into us. All humans—of all religions, beliefs, and backgrounds—ultimately long for the relationship Jesus offers. We long to be spiritually raised to life, to be reconnected to our Creator, and to live with Him in a place where there will be no death, no pain, no suffering. This is what Jesus came to earth to accomplish.

When my friend Ralph performed CPR on that infant, it was something that only a human could do. No existing machine or robot could have swooped in and saved that baby's life. It took human lips to connect to a human face. It took human lungs to breathe human breath into those smaller, lifeless lungs. It took a human hand to do those little compressions on a human chest, coaxing a tiny heart back to life. And in the same way, to rescue us from the disorder of sin, God had to become human like you and me.

Jesus is fully human, without sin, and Jesus is fully God.

Jesus chose to humble Himself and take human form. Then He chose to further humble Himself and take upon Himself the consequences of our wrongdoings. This is what Jesus did at the cross; He performed our spiritual rescue. This is why the cross is the center of Christianity. At the cross, Jesus performed spiritual CPR, and now His new life is freely available to anyone who will believe in Him as the Messiah, or Savior.

Jesus willingly became human, leaving heaven, in order to rescue us.[1]

As Christians, this is the Jesus we believe in—not merely a good person named Jesus or an idea named Jesus or even an inspiring teacher named Jesus. We believe in the Jesus who is God in a human body, the Messiah who died on the cross for the sins of the world and rose from the dead.

Now, here is the purpose of this book. While most Christians today would say, "Yes, I agree with that statement," I am concerned that fewer and fewer can actually declare the central beliefs required to connect us to God's lifegiving power. This book will help you answer the question, *What do I believe as a Christian?*

We live in a culture where many people define Jesus by their own opinion. In their mind, they make Jesus whatever they want Him to be. But Jesus does not allow for this. We must define Jesus by *His* terms and accept Him by those terms if we want His lifegiving power and salvation. The essential Christian beliefs are unchanging truths that have never been more important. They are the terms by which we receive Jesus's forgiveness and life. These terms were dictated by God, not by humans. They do not change, and they can be understood by all of us.

Aligning our beliefs with Jesus is not just about "being right." It is about being *rightly connected* to God and His lifegiving power, in both this life and the next.

Underneath every sturdy house, an unseen foundation upholds the weight of the entire structure. This book lays such foundational beliefs for our Christian faith. Miss one of these essential beliefs and your house of faith will sag or even collapse.

More positively, place these essential Christian teachings at the base of your faith, and you will be able to see God build a life of stability and craftsmanship. God's Word defines these basic truths. This book helps you inspect the foundation of what you believe as a Christian—so you can build a life of great faith.

Just like that infant girl gasping, inhaling, and coming to life, our initial faith in Christ begins miraculously. We inhale God's lifegiving power during a supernatural moment when God breathes into our souls and opens our eyes, and we respond by choosing to believe in Jesus.

We do not need to read a book to receive salvation, be raised to spiritual life, and be adopted into the family of God. But where do we go from there? That lifeless baby was given the gift of life for a purpose. My friend Ralph wanted her to grow up, be healthy, and experience a full life. God wants the same for us. God wants us to be growing as Christians.

How do we grow up into our salvation?

We grow by believing what God says in His Word and then by obeying it. It is a simple daily process. Believe-obey. Believe-obey. Believe-obey. Just as children grow by eating and moving, we grow by believing and obeying. Day after day.

In the Bible, God speaks of believers growing like babies. We begin by feeding on the sweet milk, the easy truths of God and simplest beliefs. As we mature, we are able to chew solid food, which enables more growth.[2]

Many books and churches describe the steps of obedience that help us grow, things like praying, reading God's Word, gathering with other believers, serving, and so forth. Our focus in this book is the "believe" half of that believe-obey growth process. We are answering the question, *What must I believe to be a growing Christian?*

This book is "solid food" from God's Word, prepared so believers of all ages can enjoy it. My prayer for new and young Christians is that you finish this book well fed and more confident about what you believe. For longtime believers, I pray this book is a Thanksgiving dinner to your soul—something you've tasted before, but how enjoyable it is to experience it again!

This direct declaration of our basic beliefs, arranged so simply, has been refreshing for me. I'm a chef who has been snacking while preparing this meal, and it has ministered to me. What follows is a six-course meal for your soul and mind.

So, welcome to the table. Don't worry about spilling or staining the tablecloth. Just focus on getting God's truth into your soul. Savor the flavors. Enjoy the meal.

May we all finish this meal more in love with Christ, more confident about what we believe, and more strengthened to obey our good God. He alone breathes life into our lungs. He alone gives life.

What Is an Essential?

If you hold to my teaching, you are really my disciples.

John 8:31

Visualize a car you have driven or ridden in lately. It has many thousands of parts. Of these, some are essential and others are not. That car could function without windshield wipers. It could function without headlights or a radio. Those components are not essential, but if you remove the engine, the car will not be driven anywhere. In this book we are learning the "engine truths" of Christianity.

The Essentials Matter

What are the essentials? *The essentials are the basic teachings of Christ. Remove one of them, and the house of Christianity falls down.*

Why do these essentials matter?

If you lose one of these essentials, you lose the power of Christ to transform you. If a church loses one of these essentials, it will lose God's saving power to transform its people and community. Churches that lose the essentials stall out, having lost their spiritual engines.

Who defines these essentials?

The Word of God defines these essentials. I did not invent them, though I did design this book to make them understandable and memorable for you. As you learn the basic essentials, you will find that Scripture is the backbone for these beliefs.

Why should we care to know the basic beliefs of Christianity?

Each day, an unseen war is being waged for our souls. This war between good and evil is fought in the realm of ideas. You and I are bombarded with hundreds of social media posts, videos, and opinions. In this storm of ideas, our basic Christian beliefs can become buried or blurry. This book is a weapon to empower you to fight for clarity about your beliefs.

Jesus teaches that precise beliefs lead to heaven or to hell. He also teaches that your beliefs will lead you to a life of supernatural power or to a life of stumbling in the dark.

We need accurate beliefs about Jesus, just as much as that lifeless baby in the previous chapter needed CPR. According to Jesus, we access His life and His power by believing. *Believing what, exactly?* That is the question we'll answer in this book. Jesus taught specific things about Himself, about us, and about the world. Jesus was adamant that only those who "believe" will experience His power and salvation.[1]

You don't need to study at seminary or be a pastor to know these "engine truths" of Christianity. All believers can know these. Here are eight reasons why you should read this book and clarify your Christian beliefs.

1. Knowing these core beliefs will assure you that you are indeed a follower of Jesus.

2. You will be more confident as a Christian when you know what you believe.

3. These core beliefs will form a stable foundation of faith on which you can build a rich and vibrant life that glorifies God.

4. Learning your core beliefs is an obedient response to Jesus, who expects His followers to know what He taught in order to strive to obey those lessons.

5. God wants you to be "transformed by the renewing of your mind," which happens when you shape your beliefs to His Word.[2]

6. These essential truths provide God's power for your life.

7. When you know God's big ideas, the Bible will begin to make more sense. For that matter, people and world events will begin to make more sense too.

8. Knowing these core beliefs will also help you identify pastors and churches that are accurately teaching God's Word. This protects you from "false teachers," who Jesus warned will be among us and will teach deceptive, dead-end ideas about Him.

Pluck an average American Christian out of a church and ask them, "What must I believe to become a Christian and have eternal life?" and some would struggle to answer. It's not that they don't love God. They just haven't been taught what to say.

How about you; how would you answer?

If somebody handed you a blank sheet of paper and said, "I would like to know Christ and go to heaven. Please write down what I must believe to become a Christian," what would you write?

Would you like to be able to answer that question with confidence?

Would you like a simple, accurate answer you can carry for the rest of your life?

This book gives you exactly that.

Twelve Words

There's an old story about a respected theologian.[3] This world-famous seminary professor studied Jesus and Christianity for decades. His books influenced a generation of thinkers. One day, in a crowded lecture hall, a student asked the professor a question.

"If you had to summarize everything God wants us to know, how would you summarize it?"

The theologian paused, then answered in an unexpected way. He quoted twelve words from a well-known children's song: "Jesus loves me, this I know, for the Bible tells me so."

Maybe you learned that song, "Jesus Loves Me," as a child. Its simple opening line does indeed capture the essentials of Christianity:

Jesus / Loves / Me / This I know / For the Bible tells me so.

Christianity is that simple at its core, if we know what those words mean. For example,

What do we mean when we say "Jesus"?

What specifically does it mean that He "loves" me?

If Jesus loves me, does that mean that He doesn't care what I do or believe?

In the following sections of this book, we will answer these questions and more, working through the five phrases in the lyrical line. This process will give you a simple memory tool to carry the Christian essentials wherever you go. It will also help you clarify your beliefs in these five key areas, aligning your thinking with

Jesus's teaching and God's Word. By the end you will be equipped to confidently answer questions like:

Who am I—according to God?

What is the difference between someone who merely claims to be a Christian and someone who experiences the supernatural life Jesus described?

What are the beliefs I must hold to if I really want to follow Jesus?

Do I have to believe the Bible to be a growing Christian?

If we want to continually experience the power of God, then we must have a commanding grasp of these twelve simple words and what they mean according to God.

Knowing these engine truths will affirm your own power, identity, and security in Christ. Using the "Jesus Loves Me" line, you will be able to recall your beliefs quickly and easily. Whenever you wonder, *What do I believe?* or *Is that really what a Christian should do?*, you will know where to find the answers.

In such a busy world, do the essentials really matter? Yes.

Never has it been more important for Jesus's followers to know what they believe. This is of chief importance to Jesus. If it were not, He wouldn't have packed this into His final command, known as the Great Commission:

> Go and make disciples of all nations, baptizing them in the name of the Father, and of the Son and of the Holy Spirit, and *teaching them to obey everything I have commanded you.* (Matthew 28:18–20)

Jesus's life plan for you and me includes "teaching . . . everything" that Jesus "commanded." *How can we teach others what Jesus commanded if we ourselves do not have a commanding grasp of the basic beliefs?*

Whether you are teaching your own soul, reminding yourself, or preparing to influence others toward Christ, let's reclaim the solid foundation of our faith in Christ.

P.S. You can invite a small group, Sunday school class, book club, or group of friends to journey through this book with you. Find free study questions, personal devotionals, and video messages that accompany this book at JohnSDickerson.com.

Death by School Bus

If you hold to my teaching, you are really my disciples.
Then you will know the truth, and the truth will set you free.

John 8:31–32

When I was fifteen years old, I took a "drivers education" class at Midland High School in Michigan. We students drove vehicles equipped with a second brake pedal, located where the instructor sat in the front passenger seat. This pedal, I would soon learn, was very important.

Most students in my drivers ed class didn't pay a lot of attention. At fifteen and sixteen, we were more concerned with our latest zit or newest crush than with the confusing diagrams our instructor drew on the chalkboard.

I remember some of it, like the instructor telling us to hold our hands at the "10 and 2 o'clock positions" on the circle of the steering wheel.

But let me tell you one thing I will never forget about drivers ed. The story starts with an acne-faced fifteen-year-old driving on a public road. I was sitting in the back seat of the car. Our instructor was sitting in the passenger seat.

We were driving fast on a country road when we began approaching an intersection. This intersection had a two-way stop, meaning we had to stop but the vehicles crossing our path at fifty-five miles per hour did not.

A loaded school bus was trucking along toward this same intersection, going at least fifty-five miles per hour and headed straight for us. The school bus did not have a stop sign.

As we sped toward that intersection, the fifteen-year-old driving our vehicle failed to see the stop sign. He was going to drive us straight into the path of the speeding bus.

Thankfully, our instructor *did* see the stop sign. He slammed on the secondary brake pedal. Our car skidded to a stop, halting our forward movement just as the yellow school bus careened past our car. We were so close to it the breeze of the rushing bus shook our car side to side.

That instructor saved at least three lives that day: his, the student driver's, and mine.

It's been about twenty years since I took that drivers ed class. I don't remember any of the cute girls who were in the class. I've also forgotten many of the things that instructor taught us about lane changes and parallel parking. But I do remember the basics.

And I especially remember the importance of stopping at stop signs.

Stopping at stop signs is an *essential* of safe driving.

Christianity is similar. The Bible gives us hundreds of promises and principles. They all work if you obey them. They all matter. But don't let the size of the Bible overwhelm you.

We don't have to remember every word in the Bible to be a good Christian, yet there are a few essential truths we must never forget.

Just like safe driving depends on a few basics—stopping at stop signs, for example—there are a few basic things we must never forget if we want to follow Jesus, stay on His road, and experience His power in our lives.

As I mentioned in the previous chapter, the most important Christian basics are captured in the short first line of "Jesus Loves Me." Think of it this way:

"Jesus"	What I believe about Jesus
"Loves"	What I believe about God's love, proven on the cross
"Me"	What I believe about myself
"This I know"	What I believe to be sure of my salvation
"For the Bible tells me so"	What I believe about God's standard for my life

Like putting your foot on the brake when approaching a stop sign, these are simple but important basics.

Parts 1 through 5 will summarize God's Word on these essentials. Each part relates to one of the five words or phrases above.

As a preview, here are some conclusions we will see. Each conclusion is a simple, concentrated statement that reflects the most important Scriptures on that topic.

JESUS
Jesus is fully God and fully human, the Messiah.

LOVES
Jesus came into our world on a rescue mission. He died on the cross for our sins and rose from the dead.

ME
Every human is both glorious—and ruined. We are made in the image of God but contaminated by sin. Where evil has corrupted us, Jesus can restore us into a "new creation."

THIS I KNOW
We cannot earn salvation, but we must use our will to admit our need (repent), acknowledge Jesus as God, and believe in His work on the cross. After we receive salvation by faith, we express that belief in Jesus through baptism.

FOR THE BIBLE TELLS ME SO

We choose the Bible as the unchanging standard for all we do and believe because Jesus did. We must read and obey the Word of God to realize our identity in Christ.

What Is at Stake?

If my drivers ed instructor had not slammed on his brake pedal, we would have collided with the other vehicle. It turns out that stopping at stop signs is not a matter of personal opinion; it is a matter of life or death.

Imagine this. My drivers ed instructor saw that we were speeding to our death but chose not to step on his emergency brake. Instead, he looked at the fifteen-year-old student driver and said, "Well, my truth is that you should stop at the stop sign. But you have your truth, and I have my truth. If your truth is to keep going, then you do you. You have to follow your heart and be true to yourself."

If my instructor had said those words, I would not be here today. Nope. The "Blue Bird" logo on the front of that yellow school bus would have been the last thing I saw on Planet Earth.

Jesus teaches that our beliefs are a matter of life and death

In one of the most famous verses of the Bible, John 3:16, Jesus says that "whoever *believes* in him shall not perish but have eternal life." Notice how Jesus continues this theme of belief in verse 18. He says: "Whoever *believes* in him [Jesus] is not condemned, but whoever does not *believe* stands condemned already because they have not *believed* in the name of God's one and only Son."

Those are strong words. In that one passage Jesus uses the word "believe" seven times.[1] In Jesus's world, what a person believes determines where they will spend eternity.

Jesus says that a proper belief leads to life and a wrong belief leads to death. Whether or not you experience "eternal life" after this world depends on what you choose to believe in this world.

We have to decide for ourselves

When it comes to driving, you can paint your car whatever color you want. You can argue about turn signals and other details, but *you have to decide for yourself* if you will stop at the stop sign when a loaded school bus is charging your way. That is an essential of driving.

The same is true of your spiritual beliefs and faith. While other people may spend their lives never committing to a belief or claiming that your beliefs don't matter, you must decide for your own soul what you do believe.

Even in this world, we can see extreme examples that prove the importance of what we believe. What people believe can lead them to suicide or to hope. Beliefs can lead a person to murder others or to live a life of service in helping others. Our beliefs shape our emotions, our decisions, our habits, our choices—and in the end, the very course of our lives.

For this reason God's Word cautions each of us to "guard your heart, for everything you do flows from it."[2] Our emotions and decisions in this life will be shaped by our beliefs. Our destination in the next life will also be determined by our beliefs.

Because He loves you, God says you should be protective about what you believe. Be intentional about what you believe. Filter the voices that tell you what to believe. Only allow into your heart those beliefs that align with Jesus and His teaching. This is for your own benefit and your own safety and well-being.

Jesus's teachings lead to freedom and life. So much so that modern data and statistics show an increased life span and other benefits for people who follow Christ's teachings.

What Is a Christian?

A Christian is a person who has chosen to believe what Christ says. The word "Christian" comes from the name Christ, a title that means "Messiah." This is a title Jesus claimed for Himself. If I call myself a Christian, then I strive to accept Christ's commands for my life.

Christ put it this way: "If you hold to my teaching, you are really my disciples. Then you will know the truth, and the truth will set you free" (John 8:31–32).

A sincere Christian strives to believe what Christ says about sin, about self, about God, and about the world. None of us live Christ's teachings perfectly, but a genuine believer is a person who chooses to believe and obey.

Today, many people prefer the term "follower of Jesus" to "Christian." And this same principle applies for all who claim to be followers of Jesus. The word "follower" is a literal translation of the word "disciple" in John 8:31 above. If we really follow Jesus, then we will do our best to know and do what He said. This is not about being perfect but about making a consistent choice to follow Him.

I cannot encourage you enough that you *are* following Jesus by confirming your faith in Christ and finding Christian resources like this one. By doing so, you are studying and learning to make sure your foundational beliefs are aligned to His Word. Way to go! The God who promised to never leave you nor forsake you is with you on this journey (Hebrews 13:5). He is pleased when you bring your mind and life to Him as an act of worship.[3] As the psalmist once prayed, we are saying to God, "May the words of my mouth and the meditation of my heart be pleasing to you, O Lord, my rock and my redeemer" (Psalm 19:14 NLT).

Where you have a desire to fulfill God's plan for you, God is pleased.

Throughout this book you will find prayers to help you connect with God. Right now, you might call out to God and pray these simple words:

Jesus,

I do believe in You, and I do want to hold to Your teachings in every area of my life. Open my eyes and my heart on this journey. Help me absorb these truths from Your Word. I want my thinking to be transformed. Please shape my thoughts and beliefs, so I live the life You've planned for me. Help me see myself and my world as You want me to. Help me see You as You are. Help me believe what You want me to believe. Amen.

Your Key Ring

Do you have a key ring? What does it look like? Some people's key rings are slim and serious, with only the keys they need on a metal ring. Other people bedazzle their key rings with extras: carabiners, lanyards, membership cards, mascots, logos, even stuffed animals.

No matter how simple or bedazzled your key ring is, the beauty of a key ring is that it allows you to carry multiple keys around with you—and to do so easily.

Just like we can take all of our important keys anywhere with the use of a key ring, every follower of Jesus can also carry the basic Christian beliefs wherever they go. You don't need to be a pastor to know what you believe. And while it's great to have a Bible with you, you can know these simplest beliefs by heart.

Remember the line from "Jesus Loves Me"?

"Jesus"

"Loves"

"Me"

"This I know"

"For the Bible tells me so"

Each of these keys unlocks God's power and promises for specific areas of your life. You can think of them as the keys of Christianity. In the journey of this book, you will learn to use these keys to journey deeper into God's territory. In that sense, it's a bit of a road trip, an expedition to discover the contours and vistas of our faith.

So grab your keys and join me.

I'm not a perfect driver, but I promise not to pull out in front of any school buses.

PART 1

JESUS

What Must I Believe about Jesus to Access the Power of God? If Jesus Is the One True God, Then Who Are God the Father and God the Holy Spirit?

> ### SECTION SUMMARY: Jesus is fully God and fully human, the Messiah.

Jesus is fully God.

In the beginning was the Word [Jesus], and the Word was with God, and the Word was God. (John 1:1)

Jesus is fully human.

Have the same mindset as Christ Jesus:

> Who, being in very nature God,
>> did not consider equality with God something to be
>> used to his own advantage;
> rather, he made himself nothing
>> by taking the very nature of a servant,
>> being made in human likeness.
> And being found in appearance as a man, he humbled
>> himself
>> by becoming obedient to death—even death on a cross!
>> (Philippians 2:5–8)

Jesus is the Christ (or Messiah).

"But what about you?" [Jesus] asked. "Who do you say I am?"

Simon Peter answered, "You are the Messiah, the Son of the living God."

Jesus replied, "Blessed are you, Simon son of Jonah, for this was not revealed to you by flesh and blood, but by my Father in heaven." (Matthew 16:15–17)

1

Fully God and Fully Human

What Must I Believe about Jesus to Access the Power of God?

Have you ever had your phone or computer battery die? Have you ever needed a phone or computer charger but couldn't find one?

I once traveled to the European country of Belarus. When I arrived, the battery on my computer was dead. I went to plug it into the wall of the hotel room where I was staying. That's when I realized I had a problem. It turns out that power outlets are shaped differently in different parts of the world.

My American power plug could power my computer all day long in America, but in Europe the plug was useless.

Power plugs are interesting things. Most of them only have three prongs. They are not complicated. Anyone can use them. And yet, if the right three prongs aren't in the right place, or in the right shape, then your power plug will not access the power—no matter how educated or strong you are.

Maybe you've experienced this with phone chargers. An Apple iPhone charger won't work on a Samsung phone, or vice versa. Neither charger is complicated but both are precise. Precise pieces must fit together in order to access the power.

It's the same with our spiritual beliefs. Jesus stated that precise beliefs connect us to God and to the power grid of the universe. Just as we must have a properly shaped power adapter to get electricity from a power outlet, we must also have properly shaped beliefs to actually access the power of God in our life.

Why must our belief about Jesus form to the shape that Jesus described? Why do we need to get this belief about Jesus right?

Any belief that does not fit what Jesus described will fail to connect into His actual power. Like my American power plug and that European power outlet, some beliefs might look similar to what Jesus taught, but if the basics are not correct, they won't do any good when it comes to changing lives or gaining eternal life.

Getting our essential beliefs right is not so much about "being right" as it is about "being made right" with God.

In the same way a power plug must align with the power outlet, you and I must actually line ourselves up with the realities of the universe, as God describes them. That is, if we want to actually experience God's power in our lives, we must align our wills and our minds to His reality.

In the sections ahead, we will make sure that our "plug" and our "prongs" are the proper shape to plug into the power grid of the universe. How will we know if they are correct? When they align with what Jesus taught and what the whole of the Bible states.

This chapter examines the "prong" of "Jesus." We are answering the question, *What must we believe about Jesus to receive His salvation and eternal life?*

We live at a time when many people are making up their own definitions of who Jesus is or what it means to believe in Him.

Some people define Jesus by a movie they saw on Netflix or TV. Others define Him by a few comments they remember from a college professor. Many people today take their own ideas about life, and then they put Jesus's name on them.

It's not uncommon to meet a person and ask them about Jesus, only to realize that they have simply taken their own ideas and wrapped Jesus's name around them. These people appropriate Jesus's name and brand to validate their own beliefs rather than adjusting their beliefs to align with what Jesus actually taught.

Some of these common errors include people who say that Jesus was a good teacher, sure, but nothing more. These people wrongly state that Jesus never claimed to be God. Still others say that Jesus may have been a supernatural being, but He is not the One True God. This also contradicts what Jesus Himself claimed. At the other end of the spectrum are so-called Christians who say they believe in Jesus but treat people in a way that would make Jesus cringe.

So, what is the truth about Jesus? What must we believe about Jesus to access the power of God?

Who Is Jesus?

Who do you believe Jesus is? I don't mean who your parents say Jesus is, or what your church says about Jesus, or what someone in your life believes about Jesus, but rather who do *you* believe Jesus is? What do *you* believe about Jesus?

This is perhaps the most important question you will ever answer in your life. At a time when people have so many opinions about Jesus, wouldn't it be nice if we could just ask Him to answer the question of who He is?

Well, it turns out we can.

The next time someone says "Who's to say who Jesus is?" we might respond with this simple truth: "How about Jesus? How about we let the words He spoke answer that question for us?"

The Truth according to Jesus

That's right. Jesus directly answered the question of who He is. Jesus actually made a point of answering this question in many ways and with many words and actions. One time, Jesus asked His twelve closest friends (known as the disciples) who they believed He was. This whole conversation has been recorded for us in the Gospel of Matthew, chapter 16.

In it, Jesus asks them, "But what about you? You *specifically*, who do *you* say that I am?" (see vv. 13–15).

These twelve disciples had walked with Jesus. They had shared meals with Him. They had seen Him restore sight to the blind. They had seen Him miraculously provide food to the hungry. They had seen Him heal the sick. One time, they even saw Jesus raise a person from the dead.

These disciples knew Jesus claimed to be a one-of-a-kind supernatural being. He claimed to be exclusive.

For example, Jesus told them, "I am the way and the truth and the life" (John 14:6). Jesus didn't claim to be *a* way or *a* truth. Instead, He said that He is *the* way, *the* truth, and *the* life.

So, when Jesus asked His friends, "Who do you say that I am?" these disciples knew Jesus had claimed to be the only way to heaven and eternal life. They also knew Jesus had the power to do miracles. And they knew thousands of people in their time were beginning to believe that Jesus was God.

Here's how the conversation went, beginning in Matthew 16:13.

After arriving in Caesarea of Philippi, Jesus asked His disciples, "Who do people say the Son of Man is?"

("Son of Man" was a title Jesus often used to refer to Himself. So He was asking His disciples, "Who do people out there say that I am?")

Jesus asked this at a time when many people were starting to conclude that He was God, or at least some one-of-a-kind prophet sent from God. As thousands of people were discussing if Jesus was a prophet or was God Himself, Jesus turned to His disciples and asked them: "Who do people say the Son of Man is?" (Matthew 16:13).

It's interesting in this particular conversation that Jesus uses this phrase "Son of Man" to refer to Himself. Jesus's emphasis in the title "Son of Man" is not about gender; He wasn't emphasizing male versus female. Jesus's emphasis here was humanity. Jesus was emphasizing that He is fully human. That might seem like a weird thing for a normal person to emphasize—*Look at me, I'm human.* But if you've been almighty God in heaven for eternity, and now you are on Planet Earth as a human, maybe you would be more likely to say, "Look at me, I'm human!" This was Jesus's favorite way of referring to Himself.

The disciples had seen Jesus do supernatural things. They lived in a culture where people were fascinated by spirits and ghosts, so Jesus constantly reminded people that He had skin and bones, just like we do. He was no angel. He was no ghost. He was just as human as you and your loved ones, only without ever sinning.

The disciples replied, "Some say John the Baptist; others say Elijah; and still others, Jeremiah" (v. 14). All three of those figures were God-sent prophets who followed the Lord closely.

And then Jesus got specific. "But what about you?" Jesus asked. "Who do you say I am?" (v. 15).

Now, one of Jesus's disciples was going to answer the question first. His name was Peter, and Peter was the kind of guy who spoke impulsively. He tended to blurt out answers, often the wrong answers. Maybe you've heard the expression "put your foot in your mouth" applied to someone who speaks without thinking. Well, that expression was often true of Peter.

Here's how Peter answered. He looked Jesus in the eyes and said, "You are the Christ, the Son of the living God" (v. 16 NASB).

Peter answered with a short, compact sentence. At first glance, this short statement might not seem all that important. But for people living during Jesus's time, the words "Christ" and "Son of

God" were loaded with meaning. These words were the central thought for devout Jewish people living in the ancient Near East. Let's consider the phrase "the Christ."

What does "the Christ" mean?

If you don't know exactly what the word "Christ" means, don't worry. For a long time, I didn't know either. In fact, I'd bet that many people who claim to be Christians don't know what it means.

A little confession here. For some time I thought "Christ" was Jesus's last name. That made sense to me, because people always said "Jesus Christ," just like they said "Sam Smith" or "John Doe."

But Christ is not Jesus's last name. Instead, "Christ" is an ancient term for the Messiah. This is why Peter said "you are *the* Christ." Peter and all Jewish believers knew there would only be one Messiah, or Christ. The word literally means "the anointed one" or "the chosen one," and for Jewish people, it was equivalent to "Messiah."

In his answer Peter was saying, "Jesus, you are *the* Messiah, the Savior of the world."

What does "the Messiah" mean?

If Jesus is the Messiah or Christ, as He claimed to be, then what is required of Him?

What is the job description for the Messiah?

What must the Messiah be and do?

First, the Messiah has to be fully human but without sin (or spiritual imperfection). Jesus had to be fully human so that He could relate to us. At the same time, unlike us, Jesus had to be entirely God and entirely without sin so that He could actually save us.

The Messiah is the idea of God becoming a human in order to rescue and save humanity.

In modern terms, the spiritual Messiah is not too different from our idea of Superman. Our modern comic book character

Superman is modeled in many ways after Jesus—a God-man coming down into our world, fully human but also fully God, on a mission to rescue us from evil. One key difference is that Superman was one of an entire race, but Jesus is the One True God. If we can remember that difference, the Superman picture is a powerful visual of what Jesus was doing on earth—born and raised by a humble couple in a rural setting but having come from a higher order, and ultimately able to rescue humanity because of His combination of human and godlike natures.

(If you're wondering why we need rescue from evil, or if you're wondering why we even have pain, cancer, death, rape, disease, and war, then make sure you read part 3 of this book, "Me." There, we will explore why humanity is broken. We will learn what God says about humanity and why things like evil, death, and sin exist at all.)

So "Messiah" was the idea that the One True God, the very being who created humanity, would someday come down among the humans. "Messiah" is also the idea of God living as one of us so that He can rescue us from pain, death, and evil.

The Messiah is God coming to earth to solve our greatest problems and to provide a way for us to reconnect to our Creator. Claiming to be *the* Messiah was monumental. With that statement Jesus was claiming to be God.

By the way, Jesus so clearly claimed to be God and Messiah that these claims got Him killed. Some of the religious people who did not believe Jesus was God would later have Him executed on the cross as a result of this very claim. If you ever meet a person who says that Jesus never claimed to be God, that person has not honestly studied the words and life of Jesus in the Gospels.

At the time Jesus lived, everyone in the big city of Jerusalem and in the surrounding area was looking for the Messiah. Their major holidays, their temple, their worship events, their culture were all centered around seeking the Messiah—God among us in a human body.

Even before Peter answered Jesus's question, this idea of Jesus being the Messiah, or Christ, was beginning to spread virally in the area. Thousands of people were whispering and even shouting, "Jesus of Nazareth is the Messiah, the Christ."

After Peter answered that Jesus is the Christ, Jesus told Peter he was right. Jesus was indeed the Messiah.

What does "the Son of Man" mean?

To be the Messiah, Jesus had to actually be God on earth. And that's the significance of the next phrase in Peter's answer. Peter said to Jesus, "You are . . . the Son of the living God" (v. 16).

Much like the word "Christ," the phrase "Son of the living God" was explosively powerful.

This can be difficult for us to understand today. In our lifetimes, we often hear people say things like, "Aren't we all God's children?" Or we might even hear someone say, "If you want to see God, just look in the mirror."

In the society in which Jesus lived, people did not talk this way. They respected God with a reverence most of us have never seen. For example, some of the religious people at this time, while copying pages of Scripture, would get out a brand-new pen to write the word "God," and then they would throw that pen away after they had written the name.

People in Jesus's time rightly saw God as an all-powerful being who does not need us, a being of an entirely higher order than we humans. The Jewish people adamantly believed there is only one God. They still believe this, as we Christians do also. The formal word for this is "monotheism." Mono means "one" and theism means "god."

The Jewish Scriptures, which Christians also include in the Bible, say this: "Hear, O Israel, the LORD our God, the LORD is one" (Deuteronomy 6:4). Jesus Himself quotes that Scripture in Mark 12:29. Jesus believed that there is only one God. So this idea that a God who is the only One True God could have a Son? Well, that idea didn't make sense.

What Peter was saying is, "Jesus, You are the God who is in heaven, and You have come down to earth to be with us. You have the very nature of God within You, which is required for You to be the Messiah."

Well, what do you think? Did Peter get this part of his answer right?

Here's how Jesus replied: "Blessed are you, Simon son of Jonah, for this was not revealed to you by flesh and blood, but by my Father in heaven" (Matthew 16:17).

According to Jesus, Peter correctly answered the question, "Who is Jesus?"

Based on this passage and many other key Scriptures, we can summarize what we need to know about Jesus, according to Jesus, very simply: Jesus is the Christ, or the Messiah.

He is the God-man who came to earth to rescue us and make us right with heaven.

Our Need for Rescue

If you're wondering, *Why do we need rescue, and why are we separated from God?* that is exactly what we will learn about in the next two parts of this book. For now, we can summarize it by saying that there has been a great divorce, a great separation of humanity from God. It is this separation away from God, the source of life, that results in our bodies dying.

This separation also results in our lack of peace. It causes the evils of murder, death, cancer, drunk drivers, rape, and all that is broken in our world.

The message of Jesus is that God came into our world to repair what is broken within us, and then deliver us to a world where nothing is broken. Only God Himself could accomplish this, and so the Messiah needed to be fully God, even while being human.

At the beginning of this book, I shared the story of my friend Ralph, the firefighter who performed CPR on a lifeless baby. Ralph literally breathed breath back into the unmoving lungs of that baby girl, restarted her heart, and saved her life. This is a visceral and accurate picture of what God did for you and me when He came into our world in the person of Jesus. He came to breathe life into us, spiritually. He came to give us life when we were lifeless.

When that baby was lifeless and dying, without breath or a heartbeat, only a human could breathe life back into her. In the same way, the Messiah, or Christ, had to be fully human even as He was fully God. This is a mystery in some ways, *but aren't all spiritual and unseen things a mystery in some ways?*

All who believe in Jesus as the Messiah can experience a new spiritual life that gives us new desires, emotions, and motivations toward what is good and what is right. The old desires in us led to dead ends, addiction, destruction, broken relationships, and pain. Those desires no longer have to control us—because God has given us fuller life here in this world, as well as eternal life, through Jesus Christ.

Back in 2013, one of my favorite Superman movies came out. If you've never seen it, you might want to look it up. It's called *Man of Steel*. One of my favorite things to do is to rewatch this movie and think about Jesus coming to our earth as God. In *Man of Steel*, Superman comes as a godlike figure to Planet Earth. He takes on human traits and human nature, even as he still exhibits the power of a godlike figure from another world. In the process he must choose to lay down his life to save all of humanity. The story is clearly based on the archetype (or structure) of Jesus in the New Testament—fully God, taking upon Himself human traits and even human limitations so that He could be one of us and ultimately rescue us.

Superman grows up as a human boy among humans. He experiences all human emotions and feelings. He goes to school like a normal kid. He gets mocked by bullies like a normal kid. He has a mom and dad and experiences a typical childhood. He is fully human. But when a Satan-like villain arrives to destroy humanity and Planet Earth—well, because Superman is fully human, he knows exactly how humanity feels. He is one of the humans, but he is not *just* a human; he is also of a higher order, a godlike, supernatural order. Not only can Superman relate to humans but he also has the power to deliver them.

This is an accurate if incomplete picture of what the real Savior of the world, Jesus the Messiah, did for you and for me when He came into this world and willingly fought the supernatural battle against evil at the cross.

This is just a glimpse into the depth of what we mean when we say "Jesus." In the next chapter we will learn more about Jesus being fully the One True God. Let's close this chapter by praying to this One True God, who is watching even now, loving us and caring for us.

Almighty God,

I thank You for coming into this world in the person of Jesus. I thank You for choosing to sacrifice Yourself to reach me and have a relationship with me. Jesus, I believe that You are fully human. I believe You never sinned, and I worship You as the One True God. Be the Master and Leader in my life. Amen.

2

The Messiah within the Trinity

If Jesus Is the One True God, Then Who Are God the Father and God the Holy Spirit?

In 2005 I was living in Scottsdale, Arizona, and working as a newspaper reporter. One day I heard a knock on my front door. I answered it, and standing there were two guys wearing white dress shirts and neckties. One had a name tag that said "Elder Blevins." Funny thing is, "Elder" Blevins looked to be about nineteen years old.

How is this guy an elder? I thought. *He looks like a teenager.* Elder Blevins and his buddy started asking me questions. They identified that they were with "The Church of Jesus Christ of Latter-day Saints"—a long name that I learned Mormons prefer to use instead of the term "Mormon."

Blevins and his friend claimed that they were all about Jesus, as the name of their church would suggest. But the more I talked with Blevins and his friend, the more something felt off. It wasn't just their 1950s-style clothes. It was something deeper.

As we kept talking, I learned that their church was twisting Jesus's words and outright denying some of His most important claims, even though they wore the name "Jesus" on their name tags and looked a whole lot more like traditional "Christians" than I ever will.

You see, Elder Blevins and his companion did not advertise their error, but as I talked with them, I discovered that they did not believe Jesus to be the One True God. Rather, they believed that Jesus is one among *many* gods. What was so slippery is that they did not overtly state this, but my line of questioning finally revealed it.

Elder Blevins and his fellow Mormon believed that Jesus is one among many gods, and that Satan is also godlike. Their "church" teaches that *you too* can become like a god—if you pay them money and do the religious deeds their church requires.

This all sounded like a good science fiction movie, but it's not what Jesus taught.

As I talked with the two Mormon missionaries, I couldn't help but remember the very first chapters of the Christian Bible, the story of the creation and the fall in the book of Genesis.

When Satan deceived Adam and Eve, tempting them to abandon God and His good plan, how did he deceive them? He twisted God's truth and claimed, "You, too, can be like God." In thousands of years, the enemy's tactics of deception have not changed much.

The Mormon church, and another church like it, called the Jehovah's Witnesses, both look like traditional churches on the outside. They both have books they call the Bible. But both of these churches fail to plug into the actual power of God through Jesus. They fail because their definition of Jesus is not the same as Jesus's definition of Jesus.

These groups both believe, in separate ways, that Jesus is one among many gods. They fail to rightly believe that Jesus is the One True God. In fact, one of these groups goes so far as to willfully mistranslate the ancient Scriptures.

John 1:1 reads, "In the beginning was the Word [Jesus], and the Word [Jesus] was with God, and the Word was God."

One of these groups changes that verse. They put a little "a" in there, so the verse falsely reads "the Word was a god." But that is not how the text reads in the original language (which is Greek, if you are curious).

The point of this narrative about the Mormons, who can be some of the kindest people I have ever met, is that you will meet many nice people in life who believe various lies about Jesus. Sometimes these lies sound and look almost like Christianity, but just like that power plug we talked about earlier, if you miss an essential, you have no power.

Believing that Jesus is the One True God is one of these essentials that we must believe. If we lose it, then we lose the power of Jesus, both in this life and for eternal life.

No matter how nice a person may be, if they do not believe that Jesus is fully the One True God, then they have not plugged into eternal life or into Jesus's supernatural power in this life. Such people often live a life of religion rather than relationship.

The salvation that Jesus taught includes believing that He is fully human and also fully the One True God.

This raises a natural and logical question. *If Scripture repeatedly states that there is only one God (and it does), then why does the same Bible refer to Jesus as God but also to God the Father and God the Holy Spirit?*

This is an important question. Jesus taught that the One True God exists in three persons: the Father, the Son, and the Holy Spirit. For about two thousand years, Christians have called this the Trinity. The word "trinity" comes from ancient words that mean three (tri) in one (unity).

Jesus within the Trinity

Yes, the Messiah has to be fully human without sin, but the Messiah also must be fully the One True God. That requires the Messiah to be part of the Trinity.

Author and theologian Dr. Wayne Grudem summarizes the Trinity well when he writes:

> In one sense the doctrine of the Trinity is a mystery that we will never be able to understand fully. However, we can understand something of its truth by summarizing the teaching of Scripture in three statements:
>
> 1. God is three persons.
> 2. Each person is fully God.
> 3. There is one God.[1]

When these three statements are accepted simultaneously, we believe in a version of Jesus that aligns with His teachings. And if we refuse any one of these three statements, we are not aligned with the teachings of Jesus, the Bible, or historic Christian traditions.

When Jesus summarized what His followers should be all about, He mentioned each member of the Trinity. After He rose from the dead, Jesus sent His followers to "go and make disciples." As He sent them out, Jesus summarized the most important things His followers must know and do.

> Then Jesus came to them and said, "All authority in heaven and on earth has been given to me. Therefore go and make disciples of all nations, *baptizing them in the name of the Father and of the Son and of the Holy Spirit*, and teaching them to obey everything I have commanded you. And surely I am with you always, to the very end of the age." (Matthew 28:18–20)

Within Jesus's summary of Christian purpose, He includes each part of the Trinity: the Father, Himself, and the Holy Spirit. He wants His followers to "go and make" more followers. He wants us to do this for all races, nationalities, and kinds of people. Jesus says they will be baptized, and this baptism demonstrates that the person is following one God who is "the Father" and "the Son" and "the Holy Spirit."

Jesus taught and expects His followers to believe in one God who exists in three distinct persons—God the Father, God the Son, and God the Holy Spirit. If this did not matter to Jesus, He would not have mentioned all three persons of the godhead in His short, final command of Matthew 28.

Many analogies attempt to capture how one God can exist in three persons. For example:

Water is one element that exists in three states (solid ice, liquid, and gas vapor).

One egg exists with three layers or components (shell, yolk, and white).

A three-leafed clover includes three distinct but equal clovers in one plant.

Each of these analogies has technical shortcomings, but they do demonstrate that one thing can exist in three forms in the physical realm. It is not an irrational idea to our limited minds to see one thing in three forms, states, or persons. If this can be done in the physical realm, then of course it can be done in the spiritual or metaphysical realm.

If this Trinity talk seems stressful, don't worry. The simple good news is this: we do not have to fully understand the Trinity to accept and believe that one God exists in three persons: the Father, the Son, and the Holy Spirit.

There is one eternal God, and Jesus is that God in the form we can most relate to and understand.

We could spend the rest of our lives studying the mystery of the Trinity, but let's get back to our purpose in this book: learning the Christian essentials.

When we say "Jesus," what matters is that we understand Him to be fully human and fully God and believe Jesus, the Father, and the Spirit are one God. And it's important that we believe Jesus came to earth to reconnect us back to that godhead. We know Jesus is One with the Father and the Spirit, and we don't need to fully understand the details of this in order to simply believe it.

Below I have created a chart to visualize the importance of Jesus as fully God and fully human. This chart also shows a few of the common errors we encounter in our society today.

POWER / SALVATION

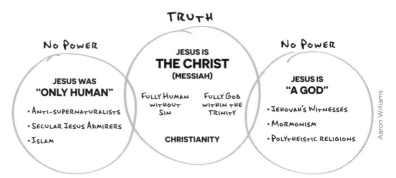

Aaron Williams

Accessing God's Power

If a belief system doesn't hold that Jesus is the One True God, then it's not true Christianity, and it won't have the power of God that brings salvation.

If Jesus is not fully man, then He cannot be Messiah.

Similarly, if Jesus is not fully the One True God, then He cannot be Messiah.

And if Jesus is not Messiah, then He is a liar and a fraud, because He claimed to be Messiah.

Remember when I traveled to Belarus without having the proper power plug for my computer? We noted that power plugs are not complicated, but they are precise. We must have the correct plug shape, with the proper number of "prongs" and shape of those "prongs." Otherwise we will not be able to access the power. We don't need to understand all the internal wiring and electrical engineering details of a power plug to insert it into an outlet wall, or to insert the other end into our phones, computers, or other device.

You don't have to be an electrical engineer to use a power plug. And the same is true of Christianity. You do not need to be an expert on the Trinity to believe in Jesus as God. You do not need to attend seminary or become a theologian. All you need to know is the plug that works is the one in which Jesus is fully human, without sin, and fully the One True God, along with the Father and the Spirit.

Again, you don't have to memorize all these words or read a bunch of books to simply know this is the plug that works! Jesus is the Christ, fully God and fully human. These were both required for Him to be a sacrifice for our sins.

Now, what are some common errors you will encounter in your lifetime?

Common Errors to Avoid

Jesus was a good man but only a man

Perhaps the most common error of our day goes something like this: "Yeah, I know Jesus existed. He was a great teacher and moral example, but He wasn't God."

This view accepts Jesus's existence in history and even acknowledges His virtues, but it demeans Jesus by ignoring His own claims to be God and Messiah. Many of our atheist and agnostic friends see Jesus in this way.

For example, I have a friend who writes for a national news outlet. This friend once told me, "John, I'm a secular Jesus follower. I don't necessarily believe in God, and I certainly don't believe that

Jesus is God. But when I read Jesus's words, I think He provided the best way forward for humanity."

This person models his life, finances, and family after Jesus to some extent. Modeling his life after Jesus benefits him, to be sure, but this friend is never going to really experience the power of Jesus in his soul unless he chooses to approach Jesus on Jesus's own terms: as the Messiah, fully God and fully human.

Jesus was a spiritual being but not the One True God

Some of our other neighbors admit that Jesus was sent from God, but they deny Jesus is the One True God. This is the error of many false religions and cults, which sometimes view Jesus as a prophet or even as *a* god, but not as the One True God. These people say, essentially, "Jesus was a great prophet. Maybe He is even one god among many gods. Jesus is admirable and teaches us great things, but He is not the One True God."

While it seems nice of these folks to respect Jesus, Jesus never taught people to simply respect Him as good. Quite the opposite; He invited worship and forgave sins, things only the One True God can do.

Jesus never asked people to respect Him as one god among many. Instead, Jesus claimed to be the Messiah, the One True God and the exclusive path to heaven. Jesus also claimed that He will someday judge each person based on whether he or she worshiped Him as God or not.

Groups that veer off the road of Christianity by viewing Jesus as a god or prophet but not as the One True God include:

- Jehovah's Witnesses. This group wears conservative 1950s-style clothes, and they often visit door-to-door or are in public places, handing out books that have "Watchtower" printed on the back. They use traditional Christian words and phrases, but they do not believe Jesus is the One True

God and therefore are not Christians on the terms of Christ.

- Mormons. Like Jehovah's Witnesses, Mormon men often dress in white shirts and neckties. Also like Jehovah's Witnesses, the Mormons split off from Christianity in the 1800s. As such, they are a false religion that looks like old-style Christianity, but they believe something quite different. The Mormon church's formal name is misleading: "The Church of Jesus Christ of Latter-day Saints." Mormons use many Christian phrases and words, even going so far as to say things like "We worship Jesus as God." But the reality is they worship Jesus as *one* god among many gods—not as the One True God. This error not only contradicts what Jesus taught but also contradicts the entirety of Scripture, which teaches that there is only one God.

- Muslims, or followers of Muhammed, the prophet of Islam. Islam is the second largest religion in the world, after Christianity, and is the fastest growing religion in the world today. At its current growth rate, Islam will be as large as Christianity by the year 2050, when experts estimate that one in three people globally will claim to be a Christian, and one in three people globally will claim to be a Muslim.

  Islam was founded about six hundred years *after* Jesus lived. Muslims hold that Jesus was a prophet, but they claim that He was *not* God. Muslims correctly believe that there is only One True God. However, they disagree with Christians about who that God is. This central disagreement underlies the history of conflict between the two groups. Muslims hold that the One True God is Allah, not Jesus. The Muslims who regard Jesus as a good prophet hold that Jesus never claimed to be God. In contrast, Christians believe that Jesus is the One True God, within the Trinity, and that Allah is a false god. For this reason, sincere Muslims and sincere Christians know that we worship two entirely different versions of God.

Jesus loves every Muslim, every Mormon, and every Jehovah's Witness, but just like you and me, they will not experience God's salvation, freedom, or eternal life unless they believe in Jesus on His own terms. This is what Jesus taught.[2]

Jesus commands us to love the people who belong to all these groups. He also desires for us to point all people to His truth and His heart. When we share Jesus with others, it is not to prove ourselves correct. Instead, we do this in love, wanting these neighbors to have eternal life through Jesus. We are called to love and not be combative toward other groups.

Being loving does not mean we give up our own beliefs. We have found the power plug that connects to the power grid of the universe. We hold it with confidence and, with love, we invite others to experience it.

We follow Jesus, who was "full of grace and truth" (John 1:14). We live lives that are gracious, kind, forgiving, and loving, even as we hold fast to our unchanging belief: that Jesus is the Messiah, the Christ, fully human and fully the One True God.

A Watershed Issue

Have you ever heard the phrase "a watershed issue"? I heard that cliché a lot when I was growing up, but I didn't know what it meant for a long time. A watershed issue is a subtle change that can lead to an entirely different outcome, such as a small error in belief that can have a major impact.

It turns out that a watershed is a real thing, and it's pretty fascinating. The word "watershed" comes from a real-world scenario that happens every day in the world. Every day, drops of rain fall on tall mountains. Depending on which side of a mountain peak a drop of rain falls—it could end up in one of two oceans.

Allow me to illustrate. Here is a picture of an actual watershed divide, also known as a continental divide. These watershed divides exist all over the world. They occur at the pinnacle or very top of a mountain.

During a downpour, when the ground is saturated with water, if a drop of rain lands in one place on this divide, it will drip down, traveling in streams and waterfalls, and eventually end up in the Pacific Ocean. But if the same drop of rain were to land just one inch more to the east, it would drip down and eventually end up in the Atlantic Ocean.

So when we talk about a watershed issue, we're talking about an issue where it seems like a subtle difference on top of the mountain, but as life progresses, that little difference leads to a whole different outcome. If you've ever driven by car from the Pacific Ocean (California, Washington, or Oregon) to the Atlantic Ocean (Maine, New York, the Carolinas, or Florida), you know they are very, very far apart.

And yet, as far apart as they are, every time there is a major storm over the continental divide, there are drops of water that become destined for one ocean or the other, depending only on a difference of a few inches at the top of a mountain peak.

This is how important our beliefs about Jesus are. If we fail to believe that Jesus is the Messiah, we do not end up in heaven after this life. No matter how smart or how spiritual a person may seem, if they don't believe that Jesus is fully the One True God, then their belief will not lead to the eternal life Jesus promised. Nor will their belief access His power in this life.

This reality—that beliefs matter—is not my opinion. It is what Jesus Himself said:

> I am the way and the truth and the life. No one comes to the Father except through me. (John 14:6)

According to Jesus, what you believe about Him will lead either to eternal life or to eternal separation from God—to the power of God in your life on earth or to a life that lacks spiritual power because it is not connected to its Creator.

We could summarize it like this: *If a belief system doesn't hold that Jesus is the One True God, then it's not Christianity and it won't have the power of God that brings salvation.*

The One True God

Of course, we should be loving, kind, and respectful to the people who disagree with us about Jesus. Our motivation in getting our beliefs about Jesus "right" is not so that we can go around bragging or disparaging people who disagree. It's not about declaring, "I'm right, and you're wrong." Instead, it's about being made right with our Creator and then communicating His love, grace, and truth to a world in need.

Jesus is the One True God; it's a watershed issue.

Did you know it's this simple?

Sure, we could spend a lifetime reading more theology, but really, Christianity is about believing that Jesus is the Messiah, the One True God, who died on the cross for the sins of the world.

Let's take time to answer a few personal application questions as we move this truth from our heads to our hearts.

1. *Have you chosen to believe that Jesus is the One True God?*

   I want to encourage you to have a moment in which you decide for yourself. A moment when you declare to yourself: *I believe that Jesus is the Messiah, the One True God.*

2. *Did you know it's this important?*

   Jesus declared, "I am the way and the truth and the life. No one comes to the Father except through me" (John 14:6). According to Jesus, what we believe about Him is a life-or-death issue for ourselves and the people we love.

3. *Have you decided what you believe?*

   And finally, have you had a moment where you chose for yourself to believe Jesus is God? This isn't about what the people around you believe, or what any church believes, but what *you* really choose to believe.

Scripture records just such a moment of decision for a person we might least expect. When Jesus was crucified, His cross was forced into the ground between two other crosses. The two men who hung on the other crosses were being executed for crimes they had committed.

As the three crucified men spoke, it became clear that these criminals had heard about Jesus. Even more, they both knew Jesus was being crucified because He claimed to be the Messiah.

One of the criminals who hung there hurled insults at [Jesus]: "Aren't you **the Messiah**? Save yourself and us!"

But the other criminal rebuked him. "Don't you fear **God**," he said, "since you are under the same sentence? We are punished justly, for we are getting what our deeds deserve. But **this man** has done nothing wrong."

Then he said, "Jesus, remember me when you come into **your kingdom**."

Jesus answered him, "Truly I tell you, today you will be with me in paradise." (Luke 23:39–43)

In this conversation, often discussed as "The Thief on the Cross," two criminals, Jesus's contemporaries, validate that He was well known for claiming to be the Messiah. They also confirm what everyone living near Jerusalem knew at this time: that the Messiah would be a human who was fully God and who would establish a perfect kingdom (we often call this kingdom "heaven").

This little conversation summarizes the essential truths we have learned so far about Jesus.

Jesus is the *Messiah*. He is also *God*. Jesus came to earth as a *man*, and He will rule all people for eternity from His sovereign *kingdom*.

This believing criminal, hanging on the cross next to Jesus, acknowledged Jesus as Messiah. He was saved the moment he believed. And what did he believe? He believed he needed God's help. He also believed specific things about Jesus: that Jesus was a man, that Jesus was God, that Jesus was Messiah, and that Jesus has a kingdom that will be revealed after this life.

In response to this criminal's specific beliefs, Jesus said he had plugged into the power source of the universe: "Today you will be with me in paradise" (John 23:43).

Jesus claimed repeatedly that He is the only door, the only gate, the only way into God's paradise, which is His kingdom. We begin stepping through that door of salvation the very moment we believe in Jesus as Messiah.

What you believe about Jesus will be a watershed issue, determining the destination of your soul for all eternity.

The Truth Matters

Why does it matter so much that Jesus is God? Jesus's God-powers and abilities allow Him to forgive our sins, to give us peace, to heal us miraculously, and to give us the gift of eternal life. If Jesus were not God, He could not follow through on the impossible things He claimed to do for us. But because Jesus is God, He can and will follow through on the impossible things He promised for all who believe in Him.

To pay the penalty for our sins (something we will learn more about in part 2), Jesus also had to be fully human, the Messiah.

As you confirm your beliefs, here is a prayer to help you personalize your belief in Jesus as God.

Dear Jesus,

I choose to believe in You as the Messiah, the Savior of the world. Please strengthen my faith to believe in You as the One True God. Help me believe this and never wander away from it.

Jesus, in a world of so much noise and confusion, help me always find my anchor and center in You as my God, my Savior, and my Lord.

Please give me eyes to always see You as You are. Give me ears to hear You and Your truth. Give me faith to believe in You as You are, not merely a teacher, not merely a prophet or one "god" among many, but as the One True God, the Messiah, the Christ.

Jesus, I believe You came to this world to connect me to heaven. As I continue on this journey, will You help me grasp the simple basics of my faith in You? Will You please reinvigorate my faith? Please give me clarity and confidence to carry Your power, Your light, and Your Good News in this broken world that needs Your help desperately. Amen.

3

Key Scriptures on "Jesus"

Jesus is fully God and fully human, the Messiah.

Jesus is fully the One True God.

> In the beginning was the Word [Jesus], and the Word was with God, and the Word was God. (John 1:1)

Jesus is fully human.

> The Word [Jesus] became flesh and made his dwelling among us. We have seen his glory, the glory of the one and only Son, who came from the Father, full of grace and truth. (John 1:14)

Jesus willingly became human, leaving heaven in order to rescue us and glorify the Trinity (or godhead).

> Have the same mindset as Christ Jesus:
> Who, being in very nature God,
>> did not consider equality with God something to be
>> used to his own advantage;

rather, he made himself nothing
by taking the very nature of a servant,
being made in human likeness.
And being found in appearance as a man,
he humbled himself
by becoming obedient to death—
even death on a cross! (Philippians 2:5–8)

Jesus came to earth as God in human form to help all people.

Come to me, all you who are weary and burdened, and I will give
you rest. (Matthew 11:28)

Jesus came to earth as God in human form to bring life and fullness of life to all who believe.

I have come that they may have life, and have it to the full. (John
10:10)

Jesus is the God-Savior of humanity, or the Messiah/Christ.

"But what about you?" [Jesus] asked. "Who do you say I am?"
Simon Peter answered, "You are the Messiah, the Son of the
living God."
Jesus replied, "Blessed are you, Simon son of Jonah, for this
was not revealed to you by flesh and blood, but by my Father in
heaven." (Matthew 16:15–17)

Jesus is the only way to heaven and eternal life with God.

Jesus answered, "I am the way and the truth and the life. No one
comes to the Father except through me." (John 14:6)

**Jesus has the power to forgive sins, grant eternal life, and save
the world.**

For God so loved the world that he gave his one and only Son [Jesus
is referring to Himself as "Son" in this passage], that whoever believes in him [Jesus] shall not perish but have eternal life. For God

did not send his Son into the world to condemn the world, but to save the world through him. (John 3:16–17)

One day all people will kneel and worship Jesus. In this life, we get to choose to be on Jesus's side now and receive eternal life.

> In a loud voice they were saying:
> "Worthy is the Lamb [Jesus], who was slain [crucified],
>   to receive power and wealth and wisdom and strength
>   and honor and glory and praise!"
> *Then I heard every creature in heaven and on earth and*
>   *under the earth and on the sea, and all that is in them,*
>   *saying:*
> *"To him who sits on the throne and to the Lamb [Jesus]*
>   *be praise and honor and glory and power,*
> *for ever and ever!"* (Revelation 5:12–13 [see also
>   Philippians 2:10])

One with the Father and the Holy Spirit, Jesus summarized the Trinity when He sent out His followers.

> Then Jesus came to them and said, "All authority in heaven and on earth has been given to me. Therefore **go and make disciples of all nations,** baptizing them in **the name of the Father and of the Son and of the Holy Spirit,** and teaching them to obey everything I have commanded you. And surely I am with you always, to the very end of the age." (Matthew 28:18–20)

Jesus's public ministry began with a demonstration of all three persons of the Trinity: Father, Son (Jesus), and Holy Spirit, each fully God and unified in their nature.

> As soon as **Jesus** was baptized, he went up out of the water. At that moment heaven was opened, and he saw **the Spirit of God descending like a dove** and alighting on him. And **a voice [God the Father]** from heaven said, **"This is my Son,** whom I love; with him I am well pleased." (Matthew 3:16–17)

Long before Jesus revealed Himself on earth, in the first book of the Bible, God refers to Himself in the plural as "us" and "our."

> Then God said, "Let **us** make mankind in **our** image, in **our** like-ness, so that they may rule over the fish in the sea and the birds in the sky, over the livestock and all the wild animals, and over all the creatures that move along the ground."
>
> **So God created mankind in his own image,**
> in the image of God he created them;
> male and female he created them. (Genesis 1:26–27)

PART 2

LOVES

What Does It Mean That Jesus "Loves" Me? What Must I Believe about Jesus's "Love" If I Want to Be Transformed?

> **SECTION SUMMARY:** Jesus came into our world on a rescue mission. He died on the cross for our sins and rose from the dead.

Jesus came into our world on a rescue mission.

For God so loved the world [humanity] that he gave his one and only Son [Jesus], that whoever believes in him shall not perish but have eternal life. For God did not send his Son [Jesus] into the world to condemn the world, but to save the world through him. (John 3:16–17)

Death would have defined our future, but Jesus offers the gift of eternal life.

For the wages of sin is death, but the gift of God is eternal life in Christ Jesus our Lord. (Romans 6:23)

Jesus died on the cross for our sins and rose from the dead.

But God demonstrates his own love for us in this: While we were still sinners, Christ died for us. (Romans 5:8)

4

Jesus Proves His Love with Actions

What Does It Mean That Jesus "Loves" Me?

I attended a strict private elementary school. Between the formal dress code and rigorous rules, the other inmates (that is, students) and I had to find creative ways to express our personalities. One of these was our intricate, in-class postal system, a network by which we would pass notes around the classroom when the teacher was not looking.

Some of the more attentive A+ students didn't participate in our scheme, but we lower-level students had enough organization to create the note-passing system and keep it running. When our teacher would turn her back to us to write on the chalkboard, we would pass notes up or down the rows and across the aisles.

I remember that our notes started turning into "love notes" around fourth or fifth grade. I remember one specific day in fourth grade when I wrote a note like this. Maybe it's similar to a note you've received or written.

> *Dear Stephanie, do you like me?*
> *Please check one box.*
> *"Yes" or "No"*

The note had two boxes for Stephanie to make her selection.

I folded it up neatly and passed it through the class postal system. It slowly made its way across the room—pausing its journey whenever the teacher turned to face the class. When a classmate finally handed the note to Stephanie, I watched in eager anticipation as she opened it.

From the other side of the room I tried to discern if she was checking yes or no.

Stephanie turned and smiled at me, so I thought, *She must have checked yes.*

It felt like an entire year passed as that note slowly made its way back across the room to me. Sure enough, Stephanie had checked yes! It was a great day for my fourth-grade ego, and a great memory in my fourth-grade life.

Now, here is a more serious question. I wonder, *If you could slip a note like that in front of God's desk, what do you think He would check?*

> *Dear God, do you like me?*
> *Please check one box.*
> *"Yes" or "No"*

Our Search for Value

I'm not asking for the "correct" answer, your "church answer," or even the answer you might say in front of your friends. I'm wondering what your heart believes. Very privately, just between you and yourself—between you and God—do you think God would check "Yes" that He likes you? Or is there a part of you that, maybe, worries and wonders if God would check "No"?

In the private, quiet places of your inner person, do you think God is fond of you?

Do you think God likes you?

Do you think He cares about you?

Do you think He would say, "Yeah, I love her," or, "Yes, I like him"?

I think from sometime around fourth grade on, whether we realize it or not, we all go through life putting feelers out to discover if we are loved. I don't just mean loved in the romantic sense, though that can be part of it. What I mean is that we are wondering if people value us. We are wondering if people care about us—if they *like* us.

In our relationships, in our careers, in our homes, in our family and friend groups, we are all asking:

Am I valued?

Am I wanted?

Am I secure?

Sometimes we seek to answer these questions through our accomplishments, our careers, our possessions, or our relationships.

We look to the people and things we value, and we often ask them with or without words, "Do you love me?" "Do you like me?"

And we continue asking this question in all the seasons of life: middle school, high school, dating, parenting, and so forth. No matter our age—whether we're eight or eighty—we all want to be loved and liked by some person who actually knows us.

Sometimes we seek this from a spouse or romantic partner. Sometimes we seek it from a boss or authority figure we look up to. And really, what we are all doing is hunting for affirmation. We are all searching for self-value and security.

We Can Really Know

As we all go about this, there's an important question we should ask ourselves: *How can I know if someone really loves me?*

The people we are spending time with and building relationships with—how can we know if they really love us? I mean, beyond passing them a note and asking them to check a box, how can we really know?

We live in a world where dishonest people will tell us they like us only to use us. In a world of advertisers who say wonderful things only to get dollars out of our pockets. In a world where people have told us they love us only to abandon us.

How can we actually know if someone really loves us?

The longer we live, the more we start to realize that love is not as simple as checking a box.

Love Proves Itself with Actions

I've been married to my wife, Melanie, for twelve years.

One day Mel and I were talking about this question: In real life, how do you actually know if someone really loves you?

Here's the conclusion we came to together as we thought through different life experiences. We concluded that love proves itself in actions.

Would you agree, at least to some extent, with that statement? If we reflect on our lives, I think we can all identify at least one time we've seen or experienced love proving itself through actions.

I asked Mel, "What are the times when you have most felt that I love you?" Do you know what she said?

She said, "John, when I have the flu and I'm kneeling in front of the toilet and throwing up . . . the times when you come and you put your hand in my hair and you rub my back, to me those are moments when I know you love me."

Why is that?

Now for the record, the only reason I hold Mel's hair when she throws up is because she has told me it means a lot to her. I would never do it otherwise, because let's be honest: vomit is disgusting. Helping Mel in this way requires me to enter what I call the "splatter zone."

Mel knows me well enough to know that I would not just hold anyone's hair while they vomit. When I choose to be with her in that moment—in a way that I would not be there for most other people—my *action* communicates love to her.

What is it about entering the "splatter zone" that means so much to Mel? Well, it's the *action* of self-sacrifice. It's me being willing to get my own hands dirty. It's me being willing to be uncomfortable, because I love Mel more than I love my own comfort.

When Mel most needs to know and feel that she is not alone, I sacrifice my comfort to meet her in her mess and be with her.

Real love shows up in *actions* like that, in the "splatter zone" of life. Real love enters into the dirty real-life stuff. As the old saying goes, "Love is a verb." That is, it's an action.

God Truly Loves Us

I wonder, do you think God loves you like that? Do you think God would enter into your messiness? Would He enter your splatter zone?

Maybe because I'm writing a book about Jesus and Christianity, you might think I never doubt if God loves me. But I have lots of days when I question God's love for me. I have lots of days when I don't *feel* like He loves me—especially when I have made a mistake or just done something stupid or flat-out wrong. When I have outright disobeyed God or sinned, my thoughts turn to things like this: *Man, I know on paper that God loves me no matter what, but is God going to give up on me at some point? Is He going to get tired of putting up with all my failures?*

We all have times when we doubt if God could really still love us. We can feel this way when we're dealing with shame, guilt, or failure. We can also feel this way when we're experiencing pain or suffering.

I have a rare medical condition called hemiplegic episodes. These episodes give my body the symptoms of a stroke, meaning I experience severe pain and lose my ability to speak. Thankfully, I don't experience these very often, but there was a time when I was having them frequently and often ending up in the hospital.[1]

When I have a hemiplegic episode, I can't speak, and I experience severe burning sensations and pain on half of my body. During the worst ones, I lose my ability to form words and my pain sensors go wild. When those episodes were at their worst, I often asked God, "God, if You're for me, and You love me, then why am I going through this?"

I wonder where you can relate. I wonder what causes you to doubt God's love for you. Maybe it's your regret or wrongdoing that causes you to doubt His love, or maybe it's your pain and suffering.

But here is the truth: God loves you no matter how you perform. And God's love for you continues when you are experiencing pain or suffering.

In fact, when He sees us in our suffering, He is a God who comes to us in our "splatter zone."

God is with you in any difficulty of life.

If you lose your job.

If other people abandon you, fail you, or forsake you.

If you fail an important test or course.

When you struggle.

Even when you have sinned.

God is *with* you, and God is still *for* you in all of these situations. God has been committed to you from before you were born. This assurance is possible because of what Jesus did for you on the cross as the Messiah.

God loved you before He created you. Now you must choose how you'll respond to His love. Very much like a marriage, the salvation relationship between you and God has a formal beginning: the moment you believe and receive Jesus as Messiah for yourself. (We will further define this moment in part 4.)

The day you believe and the day you are baptized offer specific moments you can look back on and say, "That's when I was committed to God publicly."

Just like a healthy marriage, your relationship with God doesn't end at its start date. Rather, the growth of your relationship *begins* there. You can experience the love of God on a daily basis, in all the ups and downs of life, through all the messes of your life, and in every season of life.

I have known young children who sense the love of God with them in the hospital. I have sat next to ninety-year-olds, breathing their final breaths on earth, who sensed God's love with them as He carried them from this life into the next.

Did Jesus Prove His Love with Actions?

So, what is the biggest self-sacrificing action a person could make to express their love for another? Jesus answered this question. Here's what He said:

> Greater love has no one than this: to lay down one's life for one's friends. (John 15:13)

When Jesus made this statement, He was predicting what He would do on the cross: lay down His life for you, His friend.

I mentioned earlier how my wife, Mel, feels my love when I enter into her "splatter zone" when she is sick. In a similar way, God saw humanity coughing, wheezing, and dying with a condition called "sin." When God saw us struggling with our sin condition, He did not walk away (this "sin condition" is explained in part 3).

He did not close the door to protect Himself. Instead, God chose to become a human so He could enter into our suffering—and ultimately rescue us.

The formal word for this—God becoming human to rescue us—is the "incarnation." You don't have to memorize that word to understand that Jesus took a human body upon Himself so that He could cry our tears, feel our pain, and ultimately go to the cross as a human. Jesus's purpose for doing all of this was to deliver us from our death, our sin, our shame, our sickness, and our brokenness. Jesus proved the ultimate love through His ultimate act of laying down His life for us. His death in a human body delivers us into an eternal life (see Philippians 2).

Love proves itself in actions over time, and the more self-sacrificing an action is, the more sincere the love is.

Jesus Reaches Us in Our Mess

Some religious people have the idea that we have to clean ourselves up and make ourselves "good" before we can come to God. But Jesus taught that it works the opposite way. We admit our need for God in our messiness—just as we are. He reaches out to us, and we respond to God in that messiness. And then He is the One who cleans us up and makes us "good," not we ourselves.

One of Jesus's earliest followers started off as His enemy. He was a fanatic named Saul, and he was furiously attacking Christians, jailing them, and even participating in their public killings.

Jesus loved this enemy of Christianity. One day He appeared miraculously to Saul. Jesus revealed Himself as God and gave Saul the opportunity to turn back to Him and believe in Jesus as Messiah. And Saul chose to believe.

After Saul believed in Jesus as God and Messiah, he became a leader in the early Christian church. God changed Saul's name to Paul. And then God had Paul tell thousands of people about Jesus and His love that cannot be outrun or undone.

God then used Paul to write some of the most clear and compact words about Jesus and His love for all people. Here's one thing Paul the Apostle wrote as a believer in Jesus, inspired by the Spirit of God:

> Very rarely will anyone die for a righteous person, though for a good person someone might possibly dare to die. (Romans 5:7)

What does this verse mean? What is Paul talking about here?

He is talking about the idea we explored: that love proves itself in actions. Paul is pointing out that most people won't sacrifice their life for a stranger.

I wonder, *Who do you love that much?*

Who in your life would you be willing to die for—if it would save their life? If you're honest, it's probably not a long list of people. But are there some people in your life you would be willing to make that sacrifice for?

If an evil person were going to take the life of the person you love the most, would you step in the way? Would you intervene and give your own life? You probably wouldn't do that for just anyone, but maybe there is one person you love so much that you would willingly lay down your life to save them.

This is exactly what Jesus did when He willingly went to the cross, to save you and me.

> But God demonstrates his own love for us in this: While we were still sinners, Christ died for us. (Romans 5:8)

God willingly endured betrayal, public shaming, mockery, physical beating, gruesome torture, and death—all so He could give you the gifts of forgiveness, eternal life, and restoration to Him, your Creator.

Love proves itself in actions; Jesus died to prove He loves you.

Think about those words: "God demonstrates his own love for us in this: While we were still sinners, Christ died for us."

In those words, your Creator tells you how He feels about you.

How did God demonstrate His love for you? He did more than check a box that said yes or no. Far more. He laid down His life in a way that declares "Yes, I love him" or "Yes, I love her."

When we had our backs turned to God, while we were in a posture of saying, "No thanks, God. I don't want Your help and don't need Your help," Jesus died for us. He died to rescue us.

In part 1 of this book we learned about who Jesus is. We answered the question, What must we believe about Jesus to access the power of God?

Jesus is not just a good teacher or a prophet, and He is not just one god among many gods. Jesus is the One True God. When we believe that, we plug into the power source of the universe. It's not complicated, but it is precise.

Now we are learning the significance of what the Messiah—Jesus the Christ—did. He laid down His life to pay for the sins of the world—to pay the penalty for your sins and mine.

So what does it mean to say, "Jesus *loves* me?" What does that word "love" mean?

According to the Word of God, it means that Jesus died on the cross to prove He loves you.

He didn't just say it. He didn't just check a box. He proved it by His actions, in a well-documented public execution, when He was crucified on a torture device on a real day in history—and He went to that cross willingly to reconnect you to your Creator.

Because God loves you and all people, He sacrificed Himself to rescue us from evil.

> For God so loved the world [humanity] that he gave his one and only Son [Jesus], that whoever believes in him shall not perish but have eternal life. For God did not send his Son into the world to condemn the world, but to save the world through him. (John 3:16–17)

So, What Does It Mean That Jesus Loves Me?

Jesus willingly laid down His life on the cross to rescue you from sin and from death. Now a new life is available the moment you believe in Him and receive His gift of salvation.

This means you can have

peace where anxiety would otherwise define you,
freedom from shame where guilt would define you,
freedom from sin where it would enslave you,
an identity of spiritual perfection (holiness)
adoption into the family of God instead of living alone, and
assurance you are loved.

This means you are *liked* by the most important person in the room, the most important being in the universe.

And this means that Jesus—who is God—proved His love for you in the most dramatic action possible: He willingly sacrificed His life to rescue you.

As you confirm your beliefs about God's love for you, here is a prayer to help you personalize your belief that Jesus expressed His love for you when He suffered on the cross.

Dear Jesus,

I choose to receive the forgiveness You made possible when You died on the cross for me. I believe You proved Your love for me when You paid the price to rescue me.

Thank You for proving Your love for me with actions. Thank You for taking my sin upon Yourself. Thank You for dying in my place. Thank You for providing the gifts of forgiveness, eternal life, and a right relationship with God.

Jesus, You proved Your love for me with actions. Help me now show my love for You with my actions. Amen.

5

Jesus Died on the Cross and Rose from the Dead

What Must I Believe about Jesus's "Love" If I Want to Be Transformed?

To have our sins forgiven and receive eternal life, we must believe that Jesus died on the cross for us. When we say "Jesus *loves* me," that word "loves" means so much more than a sentimental feeling. It means that Jesus willingly laid down His life on the cross for you and for me.

Jesus's sacrifice at the cross is the center of Christianity, and it is what makes eternal life possible for us. His work on the cross is what makes a right relationship with God possible.

> But God demonstrates his own love for us in this: While we were still sinners, Christ died for us. (Romans 5:8)

The Need for the Cross

If you are tracking in the journey, you may be thinking, *Okay, I get that Jesus is the One True God. I get that He died on the cross to rescue me, but why was all this necessary?*

Maybe you're wondering, *What exactly was Jesus rescuing me from? If God is in control of everything, then why did we need to be rescued? Were things really so bad that Jesus had to be tortured on a cross to rescue us?*

To answer these questions, we need a quick summary of the story between God and humanity. We will dive deeper into it later, but I'll summarize it now, because if we don't understand the story of God and humanity, if we don't understand the conflict, then the cross and Jesus's dramatic sacrifice don't make much sense.

Until we understand the true story of God and humanity, Jesus's cross can seem like a life preserver given to somebody enjoying a picnic in a park on a sunny day. "What's the need for this?" that person might ask.

As we will see, though, humanity is not in the position of picnicking in a park on a sunny day. As our dark history of wars, racism, murder, abuse, cancer, death, and other evils can testify, humanity does need rescue. But why is this?

The Story of God and You

Here's where the story of God and you starts.

It starts with God's desire.

God's desire for you.
God's desire for you to be near to Him.
God's desire for you to be in His very presence.

Think of the idea of God having His arm around you. This is what you were created to experience and enjoy—having God by your side. And when God's arm is around you, when you are in right relationship with Him, there is no death, no shame, no pain, no suffering, no evil.

In God's presence, there is no hunger or thirst.

In God's presence, there is no shame, no guilt, no lack.

In God's presence, our every longing is fulfilled.

In God's presence, all we seek and need is satisfied by Him—the Giver of life, the Creator of our pleasure sensors, the Source of "every good and perfect gift" (James 1:17).

GOD'S DESIRE

"When God created mankind, he made them in the likeness of God . . . and blessed them."

Genesis 5:1, 2

When we are fully in God's presence, we become immortal. Such is the power of His life source that we never die. Another part of being in God's presence is that there is no scarcity or shortage. There's no wondering if there will be enough food or enough space for everyone, or enough affection and attention to go around.

Being in God's presence brings us directly in contact with the source of love—God Himself. So, this longing we all have, this lifelong hunt to be affirmed and to belong, well, when we're in our Creator's presence, all those tensions are resolved. All those needs are met. This is what God created us to experience.

God starts His love letter to us, the Bible, by telling us that this is what we were created to experience: the pleasurable sensation of having all our needs entirely satisfied, perpetually, in a paradise with our Creator. He describes this in Genesis 1.

The passage describes the first man and woman living in a world that had no sickness, no death, no food shortages, no pain, no suffering, and no evil. It was a world where they could physically walk with God and converse with Him. And this is the sort of world *we* were created to experience.

But if we look around us, we see that we are not in such a world. Our world today is broken, and we cannot see or hear God.

If God created us to experience eternal love, satisfaction, and joy, then why do we live in a world that has death, anger, divorce, murder, hunger, starvation, racism, and injustice?

The reason our world is so broken is that our world has been ripped apart from God.

We were created to be fulfilled in God's presence. But tragically, we were born into a world that is separated from Him. If this were the end of the story between God and us, it would be a depressing one.

Jesus came to change the story.

As the Christ, Jesus accomplished that mission. In the person of Jesus, God came into the world that had been separated from Him.

Not only did He come into our world but He also opened a door, a gateway, a bridge, so that anyone who desires can be reconnected back into His world. This is why Jesus repeatedly referred to Himself as "the way" and "the door" and "the gate."

When Jesus died on the cross and rose from the grave, He created a portal back to God. He created an opening, a bridge, that you and I can choose to step through and onto to be reconnected to God.

Now all who trust in Jesus can be restored to God and reconnected to their Creator—thus accessing His peace and power in this life as well as His eternal life.

Our Separation from God

To understand how humanity became separated from God, we must first understand how special we are as human beings.

Did you know that you, as a human, are different from the animal world?

While the planet, the animals, and the trees all have value, you are worth far more, according to God.

You are different from the rest of creation.

You are not merely a physical being. You are a spiritual being. You have a spiritual part of you that will outlive your body, and that part of you (your soul) is made in the likeness, or the image, of God.

What does it mean to be made in the image of God?

Being made in the image of God means you are eternally valuable to God. It means your soul will live forever, somewhere. It means you have a capacity to create. It also means you have a free will, a spiritual and moral part of you that can choose. With your free will you can choose to love God, or you can choose to turn away from Him.

This will of yours is called "free" because it is yours and yours alone. You get to steer or direct your will as you please. While people can influence you and try to persuade you, no other person can direct your will—unless you allow them to do so.

Whether you turn toward God or away from Him, no one else can make that choice for you. Your family can't make that choice for you. Your boyfriend, girlfriend, or spouse can't make that choice for you.

When God made everything in existence, He made a crown jewel of creation—called humanity.

Just like every iPhone has a specific serial number, tracing back to the factory where it was made, every human has their own imprint, tracing back to the Creator. God is such a brilliant and creative designer that no two humans are exactly identical. Your iris has its own unique print, just like your unique fingerprints, and the same is true of your soul and mind. You are an individual. There is no one else like you in history, and the imprints on your soul, your eyes, and your fingers all declare you are of a higher order than the trees and the birds and the bees.

God says you are made in His image. It's because of that fact that the taking or shattering of human life is such a serious crime in the universe—because it smears and breaks the very image of God. For this reason, we choose to properly love ourselves and take care of ourselves.

When God created humanity, He said, in effect, "They will create like I create, and they will have spiritual capacity. They will be eternal beings, and they will have a free will. They can choose My ways and My presence, or, if they choose, they can reject My ways and My presence."

A CATASTROPHIC DIVORCE

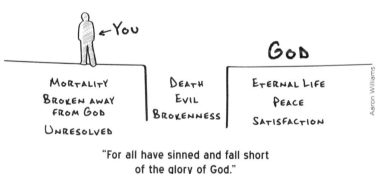

GOD

MORTALITY
BROKEN AWAY
FROM GOD
UNRESOLVED

DEATH
EVIL
BROKENNESS

ETERNAL LIFE
PEACE
SATISFACTION

Aaron Williams

"For all have sinned and fall short
of the glory of God."

ROMANS 3:23

The Catastrophic Divorce

Sadly, the first humans, our spiritual ancestors, chose to turn away from God. These early humans knew God's presence. They knew what it was like to have eternal life. They knew what it was to never be sick, to never feel shame or guilt, and to always have more than enough. They knew what it was to literally walk with God in a garden paradise where the animals could talk and where the food grew without weeds or cultivation. They lived in a Willy Wonka–type paradise of joy and pleasure and more than enough.

God gave those early humans, Adam and Eve, the free will to live in His presence or to walk through a door that led to evil, death, and separation from Him. And God warned them, in effect, "If you walk through this door, it will bring death. It will bring destruction."

But Adam and Eve chose just that. And ever since their choice, humanity has been separated from God's presence. This is why murder, war, death, cancer, rape, racism, and all kinds of evil exist in our world—because our ancestors exercised their free will and invited it in. They cut themselves off from God's lifegiving power, His peace, and His presence. As a result, their kids and all their descendants have been broken away from God (you can study this in detail in Genesis 3).

That was a key moment in the story of God and humanity. This is when the conflict and separation between us and God began.

Sometimes a child is part of a family where the parents have divorced. When that happens, the child cannot change the fact that his or her parents are divorced.

In a similar way, you and I have been born into a catastrophic divorce between God and humanity. We are born into a world that has chosen to turn away from God and be separated from Him.

When Adam and Eve separated from God, it caused an atom-splitting chain reaction—a catastrophic divorce in the fabric of human history often called "the fall."

As a result, there has been an earthquake in the territory between God and humanity. That spiritual earthquake was so violent and ground-shaking that it produced a great canyon, a chasm, between us and God.

The Consequences of the Catastrophic Divorce

This separation from God is the reason we experience shame, pain, injustice, death, and suffering. It is also why we experience mortality. That is, our bodies wear out and die because we no longer live in the presence of the Life Source. (By the way, the fact that you and I fear and grieve death is one of the proofs we were not created for death. Our lives were never supposed to be this way.)

All the pain and injustice in our world result from humanity being broken away from God. Whether we realize it or not, we spend our whole lives hunting, striving, and trying to restore what we lost when our relationship with God was severed. Even atheists and agnostics, without knowing it, spend their lives trying to secure or achieve these things.

As a result, we also spend our lives unresolved. Even at the DNA level, our bodies have components that are unresolved. That's why we get cancer and other chronic sicknesses. Physically, emotionally, and spiritually, we are unresolved beings—because of this divorce from God.

I recently watched a documentary called *Blackfish*. It describes the lives and nature of Orca whales, also known as "killer whales." When Orca whales are captured and confined in aquariums and sea parks, their dorsal fin, which on a healthy Orca stands straight up, flops over on their side. This is a sign that they are depressed. Why do Orca whales get depressed when they are held captive in a man-made tank? Because they are designed to swim thousands of miles, to crisscross the globe. Trap one in a tank with barely enough room to turn around, and the whale loses its sense of purpose and fulfillment. In this sense, when an Orca whale is held in captivity, it is technically alive—but is it really living?

In captivity, the Orca whale is not doing what it was created to do. And this is exactly the position we find ourselves in on Planet Earth today. We're in a world that is captive to evil and sin. Our bodies are broken by death and evil. We're surrounded by other people whose dorsal fins are also flopped over—because humanity is held captive by a cage called "sin."

In this sense, our sins are not just from some list of rules that God says not to break. "Sin" is a word that expresses the captivity of human nature. It describes the tank that holds us caged in, limiting us, keeping us away from our fuller and freer expressions of our true nature as made in God's image.

When those early humans chose sin, they chose a life of slavery and brokenness for all their ancestors—including you and me. A great chasm of evil has separated us from the source of eternal life and joy and pleasure.

In Romans 3:23, God says, "For all have sinned and fall short of the glory of God."

The idea is that you and I are born into a world that is already contaminated and, as a result, ripped away or divorced from God.

In addition to inheriting this contamination, we've also all had moments when we have sinned. If we're honest, we've all made at least one choice to turn away from God: moments when we chose to do, say, or think something that we knew was not in the best interest of God, or the people around us, or even ourselves.

We've known what was right, and we've willfully gone against it. This is what Romans 3:23 is saying.

So, *all humans* have sinned, and all humans are born into a world of sin. As a result of what we have inherited and what we have chosen, all of humanity is on one side of this great canyon or chasm. We are broken away from God.

A Grand Canyon Divide

When I lived in Arizona, I traveled multiple times to the Grand Canyon. This massive split in the earth stretches for miles. We often hear about how deep the Grand Canyon is—deeper than any skyscraper you may look up at in a big city. But what's even more breathtaking in person is just how wide the canyon is.

When you stand on one side of the Grand Canyon, you get a sense of how small you are. And standing there, looking out at that void, you know that no person could ever jump across that divide. Some Olympic long jumpers can jump as far as thirty feet, but no Olympic long jumper could jump across the distance of the Grand Canyon.

In a similar way, sin has created a massive divide between us and God. It's like God is on one side of the Grand Canyon, with all the life, joy, and fulfillment that exist in His presence, and we stand on the other side, in a world that is slowly dying because of its separation from the Creator.

Just like no human can leap across the divide of the Grand Canyon, there's no person "good" or religious enough to leap across the sin-filled chasm that separates us from God. We can't give enough money to the church or do enough good deeds to earn our way over to God. This is the bad news. If the story of God and humanity ended there, it would be catastrophic for humankind.

GOD'S RESCUE

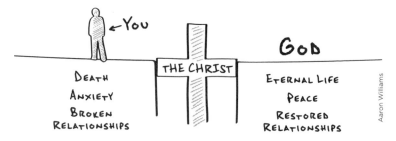

"For the **wages** of sin is **death**, but the **gift** of God
is **eternal life** through **Christ Jesus** our Lord."

Romans 6:23

Thankfully, the story doesn't end there. We can be reconnected to God. But how?

Here's the good news: when God saw humanity separate from Him, He didn't just leave us there. As an almighty Creator, He could have walked away. He could have pulled the plug on the human experiment. Instead, God chose to show His love through actions.

God decided that He Himself would intervene. This is why Jesus Christ, the Messiah, had to be both human and God at the same time—because He came to build the bridge between God and humanity. Jesus spanned the chasm between us and God. His humanity allowed the bridge to connect to our side. His divinity allowed the bridge to connect to heaven's side. And His sinlessness allowed Him to cover the gap created by all our sin.

All people have sinned and are separated from God, but any person who believes is reconnected with Him through Jesus's work on the cross.

> For all have sinned and fall short of the glory of God, and all are justified [made right and reconnected to God] freely by his grace through the redemption that came by Christ Jesus.
>
> God presented Christ as a sacrifice of atonement, through the shedding of his blood [his death on the cross]—to be received by faith [how we receive the gift of forgiveness and salvation]. (Romans 3:23–25)

The Bridge across the Divide

Christ's cross is our bridge to God. When Jesus shed His blood on the cross, He was paying for the sins of the world. He connected us back to God. The cross is the bridge between God and humanity, the bridge between eternal life and our dying world. Anyone can set foot on that bridge of salvation by believing in Jesus as He describes Himself. Any soul who chooses to set foot on that bridge (by believing in Jesus) will be reconnected to God because of the atoning work of Jesus on the cross.

You don't have to memorize the word "atonement" or "redemption" to understand what they mean. They mean Jesus took our punishment upon Himself so we could be forgiven, be healed, and have eternal life. They mean Jesus took what was broken and shed His blood to re-create it, to restore it, and to reconnect us with heaven.

Hundreds of years before Jesus died on the cross for our sins, God gave His prophet Isaiah these words about what the Messiah would do. They describe what Jesus did for us on the cross.

> But he was pierced for our transgressions,
>> he was crushed for our iniquities;
> the punishment that brought us peace was on him,
>> and by his wounds we are healed. (Isaiah 53:5)

Jesus took our punishment, the punishment of all humanity, so we could be healed, have peace with God, and be reconnected with God.

Peter—a follower of Jesus who knew what it was to fail and be forgiven by Jesus—wrote this about what happened on the cross:

> "He himself bore our sins" in his body on the cross, so that we might die to sins and live for righteousness; "by his wounds you have been healed." For "you were like sheep going astray," but now you have returned to the Shepherd and Overseer of your souls. (1 Peter 2:24–25)

When Jesus came to earth the first time, He came to build the bridge for all who believe in Him. When Jesus returns to earth in the future, it will be as a judge. At that time, He will deliver believers from the persecution, pain, and suffering of this world.

> So Christ was sacrificed once to take away the sins of many; and he will appear a second time, not to bear sin, but to bring salvation to those who are waiting for him. (Hebrews 9:28)

The most important decision of your life is choosing whether or not you believe in Jesus—whether or not you have stepped onto this bridge that connects your soul back to the Creator, this bridge that allows you to walk over to the One who can forgive your sins and give you the eternal life for which you long.

No Other Way

As we learned earlier, Jesus said that His work on the cross is the only way for any person to be made right with their Creator. And so, while we are kind to people who may say "There are many ways to heaven," we know that is not the case, according to Jesus. He, the One True God, said there is one way: the bridge He created. Believing or proposing other ways back to God belittles the suffering and agony Jesus endured to rescue us and our neighbors. Remember, Jesus said, "I am the way and the truth and the life. No one comes to the Father except through me" (John 14:6).

In other words, as Jesus said many times throughout His life on earth, the way to the kingdom of God is via a narrow road. Not all roads lead to heaven. Only one road does, and it's a narrow road. But this narrow road is available and open to everyone. Whosoever will may come.

There are bookends in the story of God and you

We learned that the story of God and you begins with a catastrophic divorce. God describes this in the very first pages of the Bible—the book of Genesis. Guess how God ends the Bible, in the final chapter of the book of Revelation?

God ends His love letter to you by saying this:

> Let the one who hears say, "Come!" Let the one who is thirsty come; and let the one who wishes take the free gift of the water of life. (Revelation 22:17)

In other words, God encourages you to receive the free gift of eternal life—made possible through Christ. In part 4 we will discuss how to know for sure you have received that gift. But here is a simple preview: you can know with certainty you have received God's gift of salvation, forgiveness, and eternal life through Jesus. Only you can choose Jesus's salvation for your soul. Nobody else can make this choice for you.

> If you declare with your mouth, "Jesus is Lord," and believe in your heart that God raised him from the dead, you will be saved. For it is with your heart that you believe and are justified, and it is with your mouth that you profess your faith and are saved. (Romans 10:9–10)

Have you had a moment when you set foot onto the bridge of salvation for yourself?

Have you had a moment when you declared that Jesus is your Lord (or Master)?

Have you believed in your heart that God raised Him from the dead?

God says in Scripture that He "is patient . . . not wanting anyone to perish, but everyone to come to repentance" and salvation (2 Peter 3:9). God desires that all human beings would set foot on this bridge of rescue and be restored to Him, but God respects the free will He has given us. We respond to salvation when the Father call us. At the same time, He allows us to choose for ourselves. Do you want to accept this gift?

It's either death without Christ in our future or life with Christ eternally

For the wages of sin is death, but the gift of God is eternal life in Christ Jesus our Lord. (Romans 6:23)

As we just read, Romans 6:23 tells us that "the wages of sin is death." That's the bad news we've learned. That's this side of the Grand Canyon chasm where broken relationships, death, and anxiety are the norm.

If you've ever gotten a W-2 or a 1099 tax form, you may be familiar with the word "wages." It's what your employer marks as your earnings for your work during a year. Wages includes your paycheck and your salary.

God says that the payment, or "wage," for sin is death. Interestingly, it's not often an immediate death. When our ancestors sinned, God didn't typically strike them dead. Rather, when they sinned, they separated themselves from the source of life and then slowly died—just as our bodies today are slowly dying.

When you and I sin, God doesn't strike us dead either. But sin does separate us from the source of eternal life. We cannot experience eternal life until we step by faith onto the cross of Christ—which functions as a bridge, to carry us over our sins and connect us back to God.

So, "the wages of sin is death," but the same verse has good news: "the gift of God." A gift is free. A gift is something you don't earn. A gift has already been paid for by someone else—and that is what salvation is according to the Bible. It has already been paid for by Jesus's work on the cross.

But here's the thing about gifts. You do have to open them. You have to receive a gift to make it yours. The gift of God is eternal life through Jesus Christ, the Messiah, our Lord. Have you received this gift?

As you confirm your beliefs, here is a prayer to help you personalize your faith in Christ.

Dear Jesus,

I thank You for dying on the cross to build a bridge to me. I place my faith in You for the forgiveness of my sins. I declare You as my Lord and Master. I believe in my heart that

You died for my sins and then rose from the dead, proving Yourself to be God. With my heart, I believe.

Help me never forget the importance of Your cross as the center of my faith and the reason I can spend eternity with You. Amen.

6

Key Scriptures on "Loves"

Jesus came into our world on a rescue mission. He died on the cross for our sins and rose from the dead.

Love proves itself in actions; Jesus proved His love for us with actions.

> Greater love has no one than this: to lay down one's life for one's friends. (John 15:13)

Because God loves all people, He sacrificed Himself to rescue us from evil.

> For God so loved the world [humanity] that he gave his one and only Son [Jesus], that whoever believes in him shall not perish but have eternal life. For God did not send his Son into the world to condemn the world, but to save the world through him. (John 3:16–17)

All people have become spiritually polluted and are separated from God, but any person who believes is reconnected with God through Jesus's work on the cross.

For all have sinned and fall short of the glory of God, and all are justified [made right with God] freely by his grace through the redemption that came by Christ Jesus. God presented Christ as a sacrifice of atonement, through the shedding of his blood [his death on the cross]—to be received by faith [how we receive the gift of forgiveness and salvation]. (Romans 3:23–25)

Left in our polluted and sinful state, death will define our future, but eternal life is available through Jesus Christ.

For the wages of sin is death, but the gift of God is eternal life in Christ Jesus our Lord. (Romans 6:23)

God demonstrated His love for us when Jesus willingly died on the cross to rescue us.

Very rarely will anyone die for a righteous person, though for a good person someone might possibly dare to die. But God demonstrates his own love for us in this: While we were still sinners, Christ died for us. (Romans 5:7–8)

He [Jesus] is the atoning sacrifice for our sins, and not only for ours but also for the sins of the whole world. (1 John 2:2)

We can know with certainty we have received God's gift of salvation, forgiveness, and eternal life through Jesus. Only we, individually, can choose Jesus's salvation for our souls. Nobody else can make this choice for us.

If you declare with your mouth, "Jesus is Lord," and believe in your heart that God raised him from the dead, you will be saved. For it is with your heart that you believe and are justified, and it is with your mouth that you profess your faith and are saved. (Romans 10:9–10)

PART 3

ME

What Does Jesus Say about Me? How Can I Better Understand Myself and Other People? How Do I Live as a "New Creation"?

> **SECTION SUMMARY: Every human is both glorious—and ruined. We are made in the image of God but contaminated by sin. Where evil has corrupted us, Jesus can restore us into a "new creation."**

We are glorious because God created us in His own image.

Then God said, "Let us make mankind in our image, in our likeness." . . . So God created mankind in his own image, in the image of God he created them; male and female he created them. (Genesis 1:26–27)

Sin has infected every human being.

For all have sinned and fall short of the glory of God. (Romans 3:23)

Apart from Christ, we have a "sin nature" that deceives us into making dangerous choices.

> The heart is more deceitful than all else
> And is desperately sick;
> Who can understand it? (Jeremiah 17:9 NASB)

Once we place our faith in Christ, we become a new creation, and God gives us a new nature that desires to live out God's works and ways.

This means that anyone who belongs to Christ has become a new person. The old life is gone; a new life has begun! (2 Corinthians 5:17 NLT)

7

Glorious but Ruined

What Does Jesus Say about Me?

One day I took my elementary-aged children to a park to play. My oldest was about six years old at the time.

I've noticed that parents take many different approaches to parenting their children in these public play areas. Some are helicopter parents who hover near their children, ready to catch them any time they wobble. Morning or night, these parents are ready to wipe any drip from the nose that might emerge, swiping it before it can fall to the upper lip.

In contrast, some other parents are entirely disengaged. These parents set their kids loose on the play equipment then look down at their phone. They don't look up again until it's time to leave. For these parents, a wild animal could be mauling their child in the park, but they probably wouldn't notice unless their Instagram feed or cell signal quit.

Of course, most parents fall somewhere between these two extremes. I like to think I'm one such "balanced" parent, falling neatly into the middle. I'm not perfect, but I do my best to let my kids be kids, to be involved when necessary but not intrusive or overbearing.

All this to say, my children were playing at this public park, with dozens of other kids running around, when the following bizarre situation unfolded, a situation that nearly landed me in jail.

There was a child whose parents were not paying attention, or maybe his parents had left him alone at the park. I couldn't figure it out. He kept bullying and terrorizing smaller kids, but no grown-up claimed him as theirs.

I saw this boy wrestling and playing rough with my son, Jack. I wanted to let them be kids and have a bit of a wrestle, but then I saw this bully kid body slam my son. Well, after the second or third body slam, I decided to intervene.

I walked over to the kid, gently pulled him off of my son, and told Jack, "We're not going to play rough like that."

I separated them for a moment, then told the other boy, "Hey buddy, we're not going to be body slamming."

Well, this kid just would not listen to me. He looked at me like I was just another one of the kids on the playground. Call it what you want—respect for authority, fear of consequences, listening skills—this bully child did not have any of those traits.

He kept playing rough with my son, so finally I decided, *Okay, my kids and I are just going to go to a different part of the park. We're going to remove ourselves from this situation.*

So my kids and I walked about a hundred yards away to an entirely different play structure on the complete opposite side of the park. I set the kids loose on this play set, then I sat down on a bench, pulled out my phone, and began checking some emails. A couple minutes later I looked up, and guess who had followed us all the way across the park?

That's right: bully kid.

I began watching bully boy closely. I was assuming the best but prepared for the worst.

For a while everything seemed okay. I glanced down at my phone again. Then I looked back up to see this bully kid stomach-punching Jack. I mean this bully kid was all-out punching my six-year-old son in the stomach, swinging his arm in manlike punches with all his strength.

About this time my reflexes kicked in. My animal instincts took over. Before I could even think cognitively, I was holding this bully child up in the air. Keep in mind that I did not know this child. I had no idea who he was.

And as I was holding this small stranger above my head, I have to be honest about something: every impulse in my body was to throw this kid, to heave him across the playground.

It was about this time that my brain caught up to my body. I was holding this kid up in the air, every muscle in my body ready to throw him, and as I realized what was happening, I suddenly thought, *Oh Lord, help me. Help me right now. I don't want to go to jail. I don't want to get sued. Please help me set this child down gently.*

Well, thankfully God answered that prayer. I am not writing this book from prison. God did give me the strength to set the bully child on the ground. No harm was done to him. And lucky for me, his parents were so disengaged that they never saw a thirty-five-year-old stranger hoist their son up as if to launch him across the play structure. The same parents who hadn't seen their son punching my son also didn't see me nearly go "papa bear" on their child.

"You should learn to play nice," I told the boy as I set him on the ground. Then I gathered my kids and left the park.

Now, here's my question: When God looks down on the playground of humanity, with all of us—the bullies, the saints, and everybody in between—going about our lives, what does He see?

When God Looks at Humanity

What do you think God sees when He looks at humanity? Is He like a parent who is totally checked out and disengaged, like the bully kid's parents? Or is God maybe like one of those helicopter parents, the kind who say, "Oh, my little child is an angel. My child could never do anything wrong"? Do you think His thoughts are something like this, *Oh, My wonderful humans, they could never do anything wrong*?

It's fascinating to think of humanity from God's perspective—hundreds of millions of people each making thousands of choices every day.

God sees the murders. He sees the drug deals. He sees the pregnant mom who is smoking crack cocaine, damaging her baby. He sees the abusive husbands and dads damaging the very people they are designed to protect. He sees the wars and the racism, the bigotry and the injustice.

At the same time, every day, God is seeing millions of good mothers who are cradling their babies, comforting them in the night. He sees loving fathers teaching their daughters to ride bikes. He sees heroes sacrificing their lives and comfort to rescue other people.

When God sees this whole mess of humanity—the good and the bad—what does He feel? And how does He respond?

Is God like a parent who says, "Well, humanity is so messed up, I'm just going to leave them to themselves"?

Or is He a parent who sees both the good and the bad and, when necessary, intervenes to protect and help His children?

When God Sees You

Let's make the same question personal: What does God see when He sees *you*?

Does God see your flaws?

Does He see the noble and wonderful parts of you?

Does He see the moments you are most proud of?

How about the ones you are most ashamed of?

What does God see when He sees you? Before we each answer that question, I think we should pause for an important observation.

How you answer it will shape your answers to the universal human questions. These are the questions we are all seeking to answer in life:

Who am I? (identity)

Where do I fit? (belonging)

Why do I exist and what was I created for? (purpose)

Where am I safe and loved and accepted? (security)

Whether we believe in God or not, whether we are spiritual or religious or not, we are all asking, *Who am I? Where do I fit? Why do I exist?* and *Where am I loved?*

We are all asking, *Am I valuable?*

And here's the powerful reality. The way you believe God sees you will shape your answers to each of these universal questions.

If you think God doesn't care about you, that's going to negatively affect your identity and your purpose in life. In better news, if you believe God *does* care about you, it's going to positively affect your identity, your purpose, and your sense of belonging and significance.

I suggest that this one question—*How does God see me?*—answers all the universal human questions.

Would you like to know God's answer? Would you like to be able to carry it around with you in life, so that in any possible situation you can know what your identity is, who you are, and what your purpose is?

That's what we're learning in this chapter. And before we get into the Scriptures, which answer this question so positively, I want to give you a picture.

Glorious Ruins

In 2015, an heir to an old barn in France made a discovery. Underneath a pile of magazines in the barn was an old convertible.

The car had a prancing horse on its grille and turned out to be a Ferrari. But not just any Ferrari; this 1961 Ferrari 250GT was one of the rarest and most valuable cars in the world.

Every year, classic cars like this one are discovered in what car collectors call "barn finds." These "barn find" cars are usually ruined. They are rusty. Their engines do not run. They are not good for driving in their present state. However, because they are rare and valuable, they are worth many thousands or even millions of dollars.

Most people would look at these cars and say they were junk. Many of these "barn find" cars have been taken apart to some extent, and so they are a rusting pile of engine parts and other components.

Most people see a rusting ruin, but the trained eye of an expert sees a glorious masterpiece with potential.

As it was, that "barn find" Ferrari was not going to start up and drive. The fuel lines were rotted. The brake lines were decayed. But in that exact dilapidated and ruined condition, with the dust on it and the magazines still sitting on its hood, the car sold for $23 million.

Why was this old, dilapidated, somewhat ruined car worth $23 million? Well, not because of anything it could perform or do at the time of the sale. No, the car was worth millions of dollars because of who made it and what it was: one of a kind.[1]

"Barn find" cars are incredibly valuable, and yet, as valuable as they are, they are almost always in a ruined state. They are not "ruined" in the sense of being hopeless but rather in the sense that they have been corroded by rust and neglect, by wind and rain.

If these cars are never restored, they are still of great value—but it's even better if they are restored to reflect their original glory and to perform their original functions.

That $23 million rusted Ferrari looked great sitting under a pile of magazines, but it will look even better when it is racing down a curving country road as it was initially designed to do.

So, I ask again, what does God see when he looks at humanity? What does God see when He sees you?

God sees a glorious ruin He is eager to restore.

In this section of the book, we will explore the ways God sees His glorious Creation—you:

- *Glorious.* You are made in the image of God. You have inherent worth and dignity that nobody can take away from you.
- *Ruined.* Like me and every other person you'll meet, you are corroded to some extent by the evil in this world.
- *Worthy of restoration.* God desires to restore you to your original design. He wants you to live a life free from corrosion; free from the fear of death; free from separation, pain, brokenness, or any kind of evil.

God tells us in Scripture that this is the state of all humanity. Every human individual carries in their soul, body, and mind both the glory of the Creator and the fall of sin and evil. When Jesus came as Messiah (see part 1), to die on the cross for our sins (see part 2), He began to restore the souls of all who believe in Him. This restoration process will continue through this lifetime, and then God will finish it when we wake up in His presence in the next life.

You and I will be completely perfect when we meet in heaven. Until then, here's how God sees us.

Glorious

We are glorious, because we are not just animals but beings made in the image of God. We have an eternal soul and incorruptible spiritual value to God, no matter what anyone says about us and no matter whether we contribute to anything useful in life.

Just as my children do not need to perform any special tricks to earn my love, in the same way, we do not need to do anything to earn God's love. We already have His love, whether we realize it or not. And there's nothing we could ever do to make God stop loving us, just as my children could never do anything to make me stop loving them.

We are inherently glorious, dignified, and eternally valuable because God made us in His image.

Here are a couple of Scriptures that describe how you are made gloriously and in the image of God.

> Then God said, "Let us make mankind in our image, in our likeness, so that they may rule over the fish in the sea and the birds in the sky, over the livestock and all the wild animals, and over all the creatures that move along the ground."
> *So God created mankind in his own image*, in the image of God he created them; male and female he created them. (Genesis 1:26–27)

God crafted us, with care, to be a masterpiece of His creation.

> For you created my inmost being;
>> you knit me together in my mother's womb.
> *I praise you because I am fearfully and wonderfully made;*
>> *your works are wonderful,*
>> I know that full well.
> My frame was not hidden from you
>> when I was made in the secret place,
>> when I was woven together in the depths of the earth.
> Your eyes saw my unformed body;
>> all the days ordained for me were written in your book
>> before one of them came to be. (Psalm 139:13–16)

Every human being, no matter how flawed, broken, or evil, still carries in them traces and hints of this original glory that God gave to all humans.

And at the same time, every human being, no matter how talented, moral, or good, is still stained to some extent by the evil that has saturated this world and the sin that all of us have chosen.

Ruined

Here's something I've noticed about the most captivating stories. Whether on Netflix, in a movie theater, or in a bestselling novel, the best stories have villains or "bad guys." And the most believable villains are those who also have some likable traits. That's what makes these bad characters interesting.

The best stories also have heroes or "good guys" who sometimes are nearly perfect. But what makes a hero believable or interesting is when they have some flaws and weaknesses, just like us.

We identify with characters who are both noble and flawed at the same time. *Why are we drawn to characters who struggle with the internal pull between good and evil?* We like these characters because we relate to them. We ourselves struggle daily with the internal pull between good and evil.

Such characters remind us of ourselves and the people we know, and they represent the human experience as it actually is. Many murderers, for example, are kind to their own children, grandchildren, and pets. And in real life, every hero wakes up with morning breath—and worse yet, has days when they lose their temper or give in to temptation.

While all humans are glorious, all humans are also ruined to some extent by our own sin and by the spiritual pollution in our world.

To be sure, sin was in the world before the law was given. (Romans 5:13)

Because of Adam and Eve's sin in Genesis 3, we have all been ruined to some degree. Every single one of us. You may recall that we learned about the fall in part 2; that's when our spiritual ancestors, Adam and Eve, chose to turn away from God.

This pollution of sin and evil began when early humans chose to invite evil, sin, and death into our world.

Nevertheless, death reigned *from the time of Adam* to the time of Moses. (Romans 5:14)

So this truth that humans are both glorious and ruined applies to all of us. Every one of us. We all have some rust. We all have some corrosion in our lives, just like those classic cars. The only exception to the rule is Jesus, who was tempted in every way we are, and yet never sinned.[2]

I grew up attending car shows and reading car magazines. When I see a "barn find" classic car that has been neglected, I value the car as it is. I would be thrilled to have one of those cars, even in their ruined and rusted state.

But I also think, *Oh man, while I love that classic just as it is, how cool would it be if it were restored?*

In the same way, God is eager to restore you. He loves you as you are, but because He loves you, He wants to refurbish and rehabilitate every part of you that is broken or rusted or corrupted.

The moment anyone trusts in Jesus for the forgiveness of their sins, He begins the restoration process. He gives us a new heart, and we get to begin experiencing His power to develop new habits. God will continue restoring us, right up until we enter heaven, where He completes the process by giving us a glorified body.[3]

Just as old cars cannot rebuild themselves, we broken humans cannot rebuild ourselves either. It's only through faith in Christ that we are saved. His work on the cross and His power as almighty God is the only power that can actually restore a selfish heart to be a selfless heart.

We cannot earn the restoration of our souls, the forgiveness of our sins, or eternal life, but Jesus has already earned these things for us. When we believe in Jesus by faith, we receive these gifts that restore us to God and bring us back to God's plan for us.

> For it is by grace you have been saved, through faith—and this is not from yourselves, it is the gift of God—not by works, so that no one can boast. (Ephesians 2:8–9)

Worthy of restoration

In one verse of Scripture, God describes how we were ruined through Adam and Eve turning away from Him and choosing the path of death, evil, and destruction for humanity. Then He describes how He restores us in Christ.

> For the sin of this one man, Adam, caused death to rule over many. But even greater is God's wonderful grace and his gift of righteousness, for all who receive it will live in triumph over sin and death through this one man, Jesus Christ. (Romans 5:17 NLT)

Restoration is only possible because of "God's wonderful grace and his gift of righteousness." We sometimes call this "salvation." It is a free gift available to all who believe in Jesus as Messiah.

Later, God describes all who trust in Christ as a "masterpiece," using the Greek word *poema*, from which we get our word "poem." In other words, God doesn't just want to rescue us from sin, He also wants to restore us into something beautiful that points back to Him.

And here's how our restoration looks, according to that same verse: "all who receive it will live in triumph over sin and death through this one man, Jesus Christ."

Just as the restoration of a car does not happen immediately, our complete triumph over sin and death does not happen immediately either. It is a process, and that process will be completed only when we arrive in heaven.

But we don't have to wait for heaven to begin experiencing the new life. Eternal life and restoration start now. We are not spiritually stagnant while we await heaven. God is already at work, restoring and repairing different parts of our thoughts, habits, souls, and relationships. Based on our daily responses to God, we can choose to make His restoration process easy and enjoyable or slow and difficult.

Day by day, God is continuing His restoration work on your heart, your soul, your mind, and your relationships. As God promises in Philippians 1:6, "He who began a good work in you will be faithful to complete it."

When you restore a classic car, you remove each part that is corroded and refurbish those parts. Piece by piece, you make the car right. You put it back the way it was supposed to be. God does the same for you. He makes you right when you receive the free gift of salvation. Then He begins "working out" your salvation one part at a time.

Scripture encourages you to play your part by "working out your salvation," that is, by being surrendered to God as He restores your soul, your thoughts—every component that makes you who you are.

Scripture promises that everyone who receives that gift of Christ's salvation will live in triumph over sin. In other words, those addictions, those habits, that bent of your heart that is not in the interest of other people—God will change those things in His time.

Sometimes God does this dramatically and almost instantly. I know one alcoholic of thirty years who has not had a single drink since the day of his salvation.

I also know many more believers who have been growing, learning, and submitting their lives to God for a long time but still have areas of struggle that may never be fully restored until they enter heaven. One of my favorite pastors is another man who had been an alcoholic for thirty years. The day he believed in Jesus he did not stop drinking. However, as he learned the Word of God over the course of the next two years, he reached a point when he was praying and heard God tell him, *I can't use you like this. I have plans for you, but I cannot use you until you drop the drinking.* After much struggle, God led that pastor to a place of total freedom. He has not had an alcoholic drink in more than fifteen years.

Our job is not to be perfect but to surrender to the perfect hands of the One who does the restoring. If we read His Word with an open and obedient heart, He will restore each component of our lives.

Here's the promise you can claim: whether in this life or the next, God will restore you completely and entirely. The promised end of that is that you *will* live in triumph over death. You *will* live in triumph over sin.

How is this possible? It's possible through the work of one man, Jesus the Christ.

A Glorious Ruin Being Restored

If you've received God's free gift of salvation, then every day you can look in the mirror and declare:

> I am a glorious ruin, and I am being restored. I'm glorious because I am made in the image of God. I'm now a "new creation" in Christ Jesus. Doing the right thing is my nature now. And where my body, mind, or desires are still broken by sin, God is faithful to restore me. He who began a good work in me will be faithful to complete it.

God has started this process of renewing your mind just as He has started the process of restoring your soul. As a believer, you are already fully adopted into the family of God and destined to spend eternity with Him in heaven. Now, just stay surrendered to His skillful hands. He will change the way you think for the better. He can actually change your emotions for the better too. And He can also change your relationships for the better, as He continues the process of restoring you.

In you, God sees the glory of the original creation. He knows where each one of us is broken and bent, but He is also very confident about the finished product. He knows He is going to restore you. In this way, God never gives up on you. He already sees the finished, fully restored you.

So what does this mean for you? It means that when other people see junk, God sees treasure.

It means that when other people see rust, God sees beneath the surface. God sees what could have been. God sees what should have been, and He sees what you could become if you are surrendered to Him. He also sees what you will be when you are fully restored.

This means that when you see your own flaws and imperfections, you are not limited by your ability to fix those things. Not at all. The Master Restorer is the one who will fix those things.

Once you are surrendered to the Restorer, He will finish His good work in your life. The pressure is off your shoulders. You don't have to work so hard to be a good person. You just stay close to Him. You stay surrendered to Him, and He does the work. Your work is simple obedience, not the heavy lifting of being perfect.

And so, where others (or you) may see a hopeless cause, God sees an invaluable classic.

Understanding the "me" of "Jesus loves me" in this way reshapes the way we see ourselves. It informs our answers about our worth, our purpose, and our future. It gives us hope in the midst of the seasons where we feel entirely broken down, stripped apart, and like there's no hope.

Seeing yourself the way Jesus sees you changes the way you view yourself in the mirror. Every day and every season of life, you can marvel that God has made you "wonderfully" (see Psalm 139). You can marvel that your broken pieces will be fully restored.

When you get discouraged about your own failures, flaws, or shortcomings, you can remind yourself that you are never hopeless—because you are in the hands of the Master Restorer.

God sees every flaw in your life. He sees every mistake, and He adores you just as you are.

Did you know that God knows about parts of you that are broken that you don't even know about? And yet your Creator loves you as you are. He loves you so much that, as you surrender to Him, He's going to wholly refurbish you. He's going to restore you all the way through. He's going to make you what you could be.

You will realize your greatest potential when you surrender to Christ in this way, because as He restores you, you will begin functioning as you were originally designed to function.

What Does This Mean for You?

When you surrender to the Master Restorer, your failures are never final. Your addictions, your problems, the parts of you that aren't where you want them to be, those parts of you that you're ashamed of, God is going to restore those parts. So you can rest a bit. Just rest in His ability to do the work. Rest in the work of Christ on the cross.

Whether it's an eating disorder, a pornography addiction, a magnetic draw to alcohol, regret, shame, jealousy, rage, or any area where you think, *That part of me is so ruined, there's just no hope*, you need to know today that it is never hopeless with Christ.

If you can really begin carrying this around with you, through all the ups and downs of life, through all the victories and the failures, this proper view of self will give you stability in unstable times. This proper view of self will give you hope in hopeless times. This proper view of self will remind you of your promised victory, even in seasons of personal failure.

It's a simple but very profound idea.

You are glorious. And yes, you are ruined in some ways (join the club), but you are also being restored.

Let this truth give you hope and perspective in every life crisis.

When you find yourself in the hospital because your body is sick, this truth can give you hope. It assures you that God will restore your body, in either this life or the next. And you will then live eternally in His presence, in a body that never once gets sick and never once feels pain.

Yes, there is still ruin in my life, you can tell yourself. *But Jesus is in the process of restoring me. He who began a good work is faithful to complete it.*[4] *He has a new body waiting for me.*

The moment we trust in Christ, we become a "new creation" (2 Corinthians 5:17). And yet, Scripture says that in this world, our new nature is at war with our old nature. That's why following Jesus can some days feel like an internal civil war, choosing between His new way and the old familiar way of sin (Paul the Apostle described this internal battle in Romans 6–8).

When you feel tempted or drawn to sin and your old way of life, that draw does not mean you are no longer saved or that you have failed. The most spiritual and mature of Christians still get tempted every day. Jesus Himself was tempted in this life (see Luke 4; Hebrews 2:18; 4:15). Peter was tempted and failed when he denied Jesus.

In Christ, your restoration has begun but is not yet fully completed. This is part of the tension of the Christian life. Our "new nature" is at odds with our old "sin nature."

When you are tempted or drawn to the old way of life, remind yourself that this struggle is universal for all believers. And actually, the very fact that you feel a struggle is proof that you *are* a new creation. Nonbelievers, those who don't have the new nature, don't "struggle" with sin. They just do it and don't think twice.

The old creation

Our sin nature can lead us into dangerous choices.

> The heart is more deceitful than all else
> And is desperately sick;
> Who can understand it? (Jeremiah 17:9 NASB)

The Old Testament prophet Jeremiah probably wouldn't have been popular in our culture today. Instead of saying that all people are inherently good and want to do good things, he had a different opinion.

Inspired by the very Spirit of God, Jeremiah wrote that while all people are inherently valuable and dignified, all people also have hearts that are infected by sin. And a heart infected by sin will at times deceive us and lead us down dangerous paths.

In other words, there are times when we are drawn toward certain situations, temptations, or people, and that draw is our old sinful "heart" deceiving us. That deceptive heart rationalizes and explains why some wrong thing is "really not all that bad."

Human hearts are "desperately sick," but this does not mean there is no hope for us. However, it does mean that *apart from Christ*, there is no hope. We cannot reform ourselves through religion or good deeds or positive thinking. We are in need of restoration. And the thing most needing restoration in each of us is our heart.

The only One with the power to restore the human heart is Christ.

By the way, this verse in Jeremiah does not mean that humans will do the wrong thing every time, but it does mean that given the right opportunity, all humans will do the wrong thing *some* of the time.

This is why our prisons and jails are full. This is why humans pull triggers, swing knives, and murder others, every day. This is why wars exist, because of the sin in the human heart.

As followers of Christ, given a new nature, we no longer have to be slaves to that old deceitful heart. We now get to live from a new heart, a new life in Christ (see Colossians 3).

As followers of Jesus, we can now claim God's power of restoration for even the most ruined parts of our lives. And we can have compassion on our unbelieving neighbors, who sometimes ruin their own lives, even as they long for freedom.

When we understand that every person is a "glorious ruin," made in the image of God but marred by evil, then society begins to make more sense to us. Nearly every person longs to do the right thing. Almost everyone we meet wants to be noble and good, but apart from Christ, even the best of intentions are beset by addictions, impulses, and desires that work against us.

The new creation

Once we place our faith in Christ, we become a new creation, and God gives us a new, godlike nature that desires to live out the works and ways of God.

> Therefore, if anyone is in Christ, the new creation has come: The old has gone, the new is here! (2 Corinthians 5:17)

This is the ultimate good news for you and for every believer in Jesus. We now have a new nature. We are a new creation. The moment you trusted in Christ, this restoration became true for you. In Christ, new life has begun for you.

If you struggle to see yourself as God does, you might commit this short verse to memory. Whenever you feel unworthy or hopeless, speak this verse to yourself.

What does 2 Corinthians 5:17 mean for you?

It means you have become a new person. The old life is gone; a new life has begun. In other words, your restoration has begun. When an old temptation comes knocking on the door of your mind, your heart, or your body, you can remind yourself, *That's not who I am anymore.*

When you say no to temptation, you are not pretending to be something you're not. Saying no to temptation is you being who you now are in Christ. You're no longer a slave to that old thing! Oh, sure, that harmful behavior or thinking is who you once *were*, but it's no longer who you *are*.

This insight can positively shape your self-value and self-worth. It can free you from addictions or other cycles that intertwined with your identity. You now have a new identity. You have freedom in Christ. No matter what areas of your life may still seem ruined or in need of restoration, remind yourself that you are more valuable to God than a classic car. He sees the glory in you. He sees the potential in you. Don't let the rust, the sin, the failures, or the mistakes define you. They don't define you to God anymore. Simply stay surrendered to Him. He will continue restoring you.

The pile of magazines, dust, dirt, and rust did not define that Ferrari 250 to car fanatics. Those were all things that could be easily cleaned up by professionals. And it's the same for you, in the capable hands of your Creator. He created planets, galaxies, whales, and dinosaurs. He created Adam and Eve. He knit you together in your mother's womb. Rehabilitating and restoring the broken parts of your life is not a daunting project for Him. It's a project He delights in, is more than capable of performing, and outright promises you that He *will* perform.[5]

That ruined Ferrari was worth $23 million in its broken-down state, and you are worth far more to God.

Your ruins—your wrongdoings, sins, and mistakes—are never final as a follower of Jesus.

Choose to love yourself to the same extent that God loves you, as a wonderful creation made by a brilliant Creator. You are eternally valuable, and you are worth restoring. God paid with His own blood on the cross to buy you back from sin, to buy you back from evil and death.

Christ paid this price for you so that He can restore you. He has a new life planned for you. That new life begins today, and it will continue into a new heaven, where you will have only the new heart and only the new nature, and where you will never get sick or age or feel pain.

In God's capable hands, your heart can be restored—from selfish to selfless, from hateful to loving, from greedy to giving, from angry to compassionate, from doubting to believing, and so much more.

In what area of your life do you most need to know that God sees you as glorious and inherently valuable?

In what area of your life are you most aware of your "ruined" state?

In what area of your life could you most use God's "restoring" power to make you new and like His original intention for humanity?

What part of the completed restoration do you most look forward to in heaven? (For example: never being tempted to do wrong, never getting sick, never being insecure, never having to say goodbye to a loved one.) Here is a prayer to help you view yourself and your neighbors as God describes us.

Almighty God,

Thank You for making me in Your image. I acknowledge my inherent worth, value, and dignity because I am made in Your image. I am glorious. God, please help me love myself to the extent that You love me.

Lord, today I remind myself that all people are inherently valuable and dignified because all humans are made in Your image. Lord, this includes the people who hurt me and make me feel uncomfortable. Help me love even those people, trusting that You can restore them too.

Jesus, I thank You for being a Master Restorer. I thank You that You have the power to wash away what is ruined and to restore me. Thank You for coming into my life. Thank You for beginning Your restoration work in me. Jesus, I invite You to continue restoring and rehabilitating every area of my life.

Lord, I claim your promise that "He who began a good work will be faithful to complete it" (Philippians 1:6). I surrender myself into Your hands and ask You to continue Your work. I give You permission to fix and change any part of me.

Help me live from this new nature. I want to function, think, act, and feel as You intended and designed me to—in complete spiritual, emotional, and physical health. I thank You that You are now restoring me. I give You access and control of every area of my thoughts, habits, body, and being, so that You can continue Your restoration work. Amen.

8

Being Restored the Moment You Believe

How Do I Live as a "New Creation"?
How Can I Better Understand Myself and Other People?

For all who believe in Christ, the restoration of our souls has begun. "This means that anyone who belongs to Christ has become a new person. The old life is gone; a new life has begun!" (2 Corinthians 5:17 NLT).

Whether we are living it out or not, everyone who "belongs to Christ" is a new creation.

So, how do we begin being ourselves?

How do we begin living as the new creations that we are?

I grew up in Michigan, the home of the American automobile industry. During my elementary years, I became a car fanatic. Every square foot of my bedroom walls was covered with pictures of cars I had cut from various magazines and taped up.

For Christmas and birthday presents, I always asked for car magazine subscriptions and car models. Sometimes I joke that I would not know how to read today had it not been for *Motor Trend*, *Car and Driver*, and *Hot Rod* magazines.

As I rode my BMX bike around the neighborhood, I often stopped when I would see a garage door open and an old car being restored inside. These restoration projects were typically the work of retiree-aged guys, and most were kind enough to welcome me in where I could see the project. I was fascinated with every nut and bolt, the frames, the engines, the many components.

I got to spend a lot of time in those garages. When a "glorious ruin" would arrive on a trailer, some rusted and unmoving barn find of a car, these guys would let me help them disassemble it.

To get started, we would remove every single part from a car that was being restored, and I mean every part. While old cars are simpler than today's automobiles, even these vintage vehicles would have thousands of pieces. In such a restoration, every single piece got cleaned up. Every single part got refurbished and repainted.

One by one, the parts would be restored. If the piece was metal, it would go through a sandblaster that would strip away all the rust, debris, and old paint. Then, after it was clean metal, it would be primed and painted.

Old broken glass would come out to be replaced with new glass. Old chrome would be re-chromed. Old rubber—rotted and falling apart—would be tossed into the trash to be replaced with brand-new rubber seals.

Piece by piece, these old cars would be cleaned up.

This is what God is in the process of doing with us. Until we leave this earth and go to heaven, we are restoration works in progress.

What does this mean in real life? Let's consider another true restoration story.

A family in England once decided to get rid of an old wreck of a car that had been rusting in their backyard. It was largely taken apart. The engine lay under a tarp and some decomposing leaves. The front of the car lacked any body panels, and with that missing engine it looked more like a trailer—just two rotting rubber tires sticking up from a heap of rusted metal.

Most people would have looked at that metal and said, "It's a ruin. Why bother?" then called for a junkyard to pick it up as scrap. But that dilapidated and disassembled car was a Jaguar worth about $80,000 just as it sat, with its engine and other parts scattered around the yard.

When you feel like you're a hopeless cause with your problems (I know I certainly feel that way sometimes), I want you to picture a perfectly restored automobile in better-than-new condition. That car in England required three thousand hours of restoration work, but it was transformed from ruined to glorious. (See visuals of this car at JohnSDickerson.com/media.)

The transformation of this car is just a little picture of God's plans for you. When God sees humanity, He sees our brokenness, He sees our problems—but He also sees the potential of what can be. Car collectors spend millions of dollars to purchase and restore these "glorious ruin" classics. When someone knows the value of something, they'll pay a great cost for it.

Worth It

We learned in part 2 about the cost God paid when Jesus died on the cross to restore us, redeem us, and reconnect us. Now, as we surrender to God, He continues restoring us. He has the finished result in mind already.

And here's how this works in your Christian life. Your work is not trying to be perfect but rather staying close to the Restorer. Keep trusting Him, and He will align your circumstances and even your emotions so that He can keep refurbishing different parts of you.

This is not to say you won't feel any pain. As a kid, I often squeezed my eyes closed and plugged my ears when a worker would take a power sander or air-powered drill to some old rusted part of a car. I felt like the car must be in pain while it was being taken apart, and I have felt like that when God really works on an area in my life.

But it's always worth it. The pain of the restoration is temporary. The final product is forever.

As beautiful as that fully restored Jaguar looks, the three thousand hours of work to transform that car included many times when sparks flew because metal was being ground down. Lots of shaving, cutting, and sanding. Sometimes, when God is really restoring us, it hurts in the moment. But the end result is worth it.

For a while, God may work on your pride. Then, just when you think you can't handle it anymore, God might set that down and begin to work on your lust. Then, when you can't handle that anymore, He might start to work on your relationships, and then He'll come back to that pride. He's sanding. He's repainting. He's refurbishing. He's disassembling and reassembling. He's in the process. You are a glorious ruin, and you are being restored.

I encourage you to keep surrendering to the hands of the Restorer. His work can be painful. But His results are beautiful.

In Ephesians 2:10, God describes you as His masterpiece, a crafted *poema*; that's the Greek word from which we get our word "poem." In eternity, we who trust the Master to restore us will be a museum of sorts, on display to declare that He is not only the mightiest being in the universe, not only the brilliant Creator but also the most capable Redeemer, one who restores when evil has destroyed. My friend Victor is a Porsche mechanic, a specialist who restores a certain type of Porsche. He graduated from Porsche University in Germany, where he studied a specific year range of air-cooled Porsches.

These days, for his full-time job, Victor restores two or three Porsches a year. These are really high-end restorations. By the time he is finished restoring a vintage Porsche, the car looks and drives like it did when it first rolled out of the factory in Germany many decades ago.

I've had the opportunity to see some of Victor's restorations and when you look at one of those restored Porsches, you can see the surgical precision Victor uses. Just within the top half of the motor, there are hundreds of parts. Victor will take off every single part. With great love and care and precision, he will completely refurbish every bolt, every screw, every spring, every component, before he reassembles the car.

Most experts, when they restore a car, begin with the engine. That's because the engine is the heart of the car.

This is also where God starts restoring us. He starts with our hearts. God starts changing us on the inside. Victor could be eight months into working on a Porsche, and if you walked into his shop, the car's exterior would still look all rusty and beat up. The dashboard might still have places where mice had chewed it up when it was neglected.

In those times, someone who doesn't understand the process might look at the beat-up Porsche body and conclude that Victor is not getting much work done. But the process is intentional. And the reality is that the engine and other parts take a lot more time than the body or the dashboard.

Just as Victor sometimes saves the exterior for last when he is restoring a Porsche, so it is with us. Our bodies are the last thing God will restore on us, a moment God describes in 2 Corinthians 5. The restoration of our hearts, minds, habits, and other components begins in this life. But the complete restoration of our bodies will not happen until we leave this world and wake up in heaven.

During our years on Planet Earth, in this lifetime, God works most on restoring our insides. Then, when we breathe our final breath, we are going to wake up in a brand-new body. We will be completely new. If you've dealt with chronic sickness, pain, or disease, this is a glorious moment to anticipate.

We learned in the last chapter that the moment we trust in Christ we become a "new creation." That's a powerful truth we can experience a little bit more every day between now and heaven.

But as we also learned, from the prophet Jeremiah, our hearts are "deceitful above all things." If your experience is anything like mine, you will find that your old sin nature and your old heart will still tempt you toward sin and evil every day. Yet here is one of the matters that separate followers of Jesus from everyone else in our culture today: when our hearts tell us to do something God calls "sin," we choose to not follow our hearts. At least, this is what we strive toward.

"Follow Your Heart"

In the last thirty years, "Follow your heart" has become a tired and popular cliché. It sounds cute. Sometimes it's inspiring. But the sad underbelly of this principle is that our young people are often not warned about the times when their hearts may deceive them. There will be days when their hearts tell them to do something stupid, painful, or even outright evil.

In a very sick way, every school shooter who takes a gun into their school was, in that moment, "following their heart" as they acted out a heinous evil.

In the last ten years, suicide has become the fastest growing cause of death for young people in America. Sadly, many times, in a moment of depression or discouragement, these young people are simply "following their heart."

I will say here—based on the Word of God—what may not be popular in our time: if your heart ever tells you to harm yourself or someone else, then please, please, please do not follow your heart.

I cannot say it more emphatically. *If your heart tells you to harm or do evil—to yourself or anyone else—then absolutely do not listen.*

According to our Maker and His Word, the Bible, our hearts can have moments of glory and nobility—but those same hearts will have moments of depression, discouragement, and sinfulness. Your heart will at times deceive you into harming yourself or others, maybe not as dramatically as the examples above but more likely through addiction or a moment of selfishness that betrays someone who trusted you.

The old Christian word for this sinfulness of heart was "depravity." Every person carries around the glory of God in their being, and every person also carries around a beating heart that longs for nobility but is crippled by depravity. Depravity is a key concept in understanding human nature. While humans are always glorious and have inherent dignity, all humans also have this bent to do wrong at times.

I know that popular advice to "follow your heart" is often well intentioned. The people giving that advice are likely thinking about the good part of the heart. But, here's the thing: I know just from living inside my head that if I followed my heart, I would be in jail today. If I followed my heart, it would lead me to betray people. My heart would lead me to lie on my taxes. My heart, some days, would lead me to cheat on my spouse. My heart would lead me to make selfish choices that would harm my children and many other people who depend on me.

And if I can be really honest, when somebody cuts me off in traffic and I experience road rage, my heart would lead me to run them off the road. Thank God, I have not always followed my heart.

No, in the moments when our hearts suggest anything that contradicts God's Word, we must do ourselves a favor and not follow them.

Remember that bully kid who was beating up my six-year-old son? Now, if I had "followed my heart" in that situation, that kid would have gotten thrown across the park, and I would probably be in prison today. It's a good thing I didn't follow my heart in that situation. And if you're honest, you know it's a good thing you have not followed your heart in some situations too.

Learn to Discern

We all have those moments. The most noble human beings, our greatest heroes, will at certain moments, at certain times, do what is not right. However, when we trust in Christ, He gives us the ability to discern what is good and what is bad. Jeremiah 17:9 puts it this way: "The heart is more deceitful than all else and is desperately sick; who can understand it?" (NASB).

Rather than our own hearts being the standard of what is right or wrong, the Word of God becomes our standard. Rather than our own feelings or our neighbor's feelings telling us who we are or what our identity is, what God says about us becomes the definition of our identity.

Your heart is capable of great good, but your heart is also capable of great harm to yourself or others. As you allow God to restore you and renew your mind, He can reduce the harmful part of your heart and shine up and fully restore the parts of your heart that are noble and desire to help others.

God wants to help you discern which desires of your heart will lead to life and which will lead to death. The two primary discerning vehicles God gives you are His Word, which we will study in part 5, and His Spirit, which we will study in part 6. God gives these two gifts to all believers to steer our hearts toward the desires that are godly and to help us say no to the desires that are not godly.[1]

Let me give you a parenting implication here. I'm a millennial currently raising elementary-aged children. In my generation, it's common to hear parents and speakers say, "Just nurture your child's every desire. Encourage them to follow their hearts no matter what, and they can be whatever they want to be as long as they follow their hearts."

Now, here's the thing. I have wonderful kids, and they are very glorious, but I have found my cute, sweet child biting the face of my other child. In that moment, should I tell her, "Oh, honey, just keep following your heart. You could be the best face-biter the world has ever seen. Don't let anyone tell you what you can and can't do. You follow that heart and become the best face-biter of all time!"?

Good parenting is not telling our children to follow their every desire. Good parenting is teaching our children which desires are noble and which are evil—which desires are glorious and which are ruinous.

Our job as parents is to teach our children which desires will make them a great person and which will land them in jail or destroy their future marriage. It's not very good parenting to pretend a destructive and dangerous pattern of the heart is a good thing.

In the same way, our Good Father, God, wants to parent us. There are many good desires He has placed in us that He wants us to follow. He wants to teach us how to sort through our desires— the ones that are glorious and worthy and those that lead us to pain and destruction.

The Bible says that because of our "depravity," we are slaves to sin. That is, apart from Christ we are powerless to say no to sin. Apart from Christ, our eyes are blinded spiritually. In other words, we may know some right and wrong, but we don't know right and wrong perfectly. Just like an old car, we might kind of roll, but we don't run perfectly.

When we believe in Christ, we do not immediately become perfect in our choices. However, the blinders get removed from our eyes. God supernaturally removes the chains of sin. As a result, now we have the capability to see the right option when we couldn't see it before. We are no longer slaves to sin or fear, and we have the freedom to do what is right.[2]

We can now amplify our glorious impulses and identify our ruinous ones.

In Colossians 3:1, God tells us "Now that you are raised with Christ, you are a new creation. You have a new mind and a new heart."[3] Then, just like restoring a car, God instructs us in exactly which components to take off and how to replace them with new components.

We take off different things from our broken, harmful, sinful nature and then put on good new things from the new nature of God within us. For example, God will say, "Take off sexual immorality. Take off filthy language. Take off lying to one another."

Now, is God giving you those commands because He doesn't love you and doesn't want you to be true to your heart?

No, He's telling you those things because He *does* love you, and He wants you to be safe. He wants to help you become what you can actually be. He loves you when you are rusting in a junkyard, but He loves you enough to say, "Take off those old parts, and put on these new parts like kindness, compassion, gentleness. Put on self-control, and over all of that, put on love."

God gives us a number of these before-and-after lists in the New Testament. Each one shows us which old parts to take off and which new parts to put on. (In part 6 we will discuss where to find the power to do all this work when we feel we can't actually do it.)

Colossians 3

Take Off	Put On
Sexual immorality	The new self
Impurity	An identity as God's chosen
Lust	An identity that is "holy
Evil desires	and dearly loved"
Greed	Compassion
Idolatry	Kindness
Anger	Humility
Rage	Gentleness
Malice	Patience
Slander	Forgiveness
Filthy language	Love
Lying	Unity
	The peace of Christ
	Gratitude

1 Peter 2

Take Off	Put On
Malice	A desire for under-
Deceit	standing the basics of
Hypocrisy	God's Word
Envy	A longing to grow in
Slander of every kind	your salvation

Ephesians 5

Take Off	Put On
Sexual immorality	Walking in the way of love
Impurity	Giving thanks to God
Greed	Encouraging other
Obscenity	believers
Foolish talk	Singing songs related to
Dirty joking	Scripture

As you walk with Christ and read His Word, He will give you the ability to discern whether an impulse or desire is pleasing to Him or not. When my impulse is to take from another person, for example, that's an impulse I am going to starve, and I'm going to remove it.

Part of being a "new creation" is that God restores your will so that you can say yes to godly choices when you previously could not. God also restores your will so that you can say no to ungodly choices when previously you did not have the power to resist those things.

When you trust in Christ, you are set free to love as you were designed to love.

I mentioned how my friend Victor, the Porsche restorer, begins his work first on the engine of the car. After that he does a "frame-off" restoration. That means he removes every part of the car from the steel frame. And then he refurbishes every system: the brakes, the cooling system, the electrical, and everything else.

In our lifetimes, God will similarly refurbish our hearts, our various emotions, our habits, and our thoughts. The final thing

God will restore is our bodies. In this world broken by sin, our bodies will deteriorate as we age.

Sure, even in its fallen and ruined state, your body is glorious. The way it heals itself. The intricacies of its systems. I could go on. However, your body, like mine, is prone to sickness and disease. Our bodies are ruined by the evil Adam and Eve unleashed on all people. The fall of sin is why we ultimately die.[4]

We live in this "ruined" world knowing it is not our end. We are passing through the pain. We daily claim the hope that God is working on the inside of us, and we anticipate that our final breath here on earth will lead us to wake up in our glorified bodies in heaven.

Living This Out

If Scripture tells me to "take off" the old nature and to "put on" the new nature, how do I do that? This is a lifelong process. We all have "old" sins we've taken off years ago and forgotten about that sometimes sneak up and surprise us. We work at them continually, and that's why we all need a church family or team of other believers to encourage us and keep us moving ahead.

Scripture tells us to "work out [our] salvation" (Philippians 2:12) with reverence for God. Some believers read that verse and place a heavy burden upon themselves, thinking they have to become like God by "working out" their salvation in their own effort.

More positively, I know other believers who experience this same instruction to "work out [our] salvation" with joy. These believers are people who understand that their salvation depends on God and not on themselves. They have joy in understanding that only God's hands can do the regenerating of our nature and the restoration of our components.

Our "work" is simply to "abide" in Him, as Jesus taught in John 15:4–6 (NASB). When we make it our work to stay close to Christ in our hearts and minds, then we allow *Him* to continue doing the heavy lifting in our lives. (Staying submitted to Him as He works on us is not always easy, which is why it's called work.)

How do you abide in Christ so that He can continue restoring you?

This abiding begins in your heart. It is about seeking to know Christ and live His way. The very fact that you're reading this book indicates that your heart is doing this, *right now*. You also work out your salvation by:

- reading God's Word and applying it regularly,
- submitting yourself to God in daily prayer,
- regularly confessing the sin choices you make in rebellion to God (you can claim 1 John 1:8–9 as you do),
- learning to walk in the Spirit (see part 6 of this book), and
- gathering to worship with other believers. God calls this "not forsaking" (Hebrews 10:25 NASB) the gathering of believers who inspire, challenge, and motivate you to live up to your calling as a follower of Christ. We often call this "church," and it is God's will for you to be part of a Bible-believing church (or gathering of believers) that lifts Christ high and teaches the Word of God.

There Is Hope

What does this restoration process mean? It means you are never hopeless, and it means Christ is the only One who can restore your broken parts. These things we've learned about human nature are true in all of us. They are true of our children, true in our families, and true in every human society.

As followers of Jesus, we know the solution to the human condition. How exciting! What a hope we get to share with the world.

Can you imagine living in a society where every person is allowing Christ to restore them?

Can you imagine being in a family where every person views the others as gloriously made in God's image and worthy of restoration?

Can you imagine a home where every parent and child values and dignifies each other—even in the worst moments?

Imagine a home where the thinking runs like this: "I understand parts of you are broken, because there are parts of me that are broken too, but I am hopeful with you. When you have a broken part, and it's affecting everyone else who lives in the house, we're all cheering you on. God can restore that part of you, just like He is restoring parts of me."

Between you and God, if there was one part of you that God could restore right now, one part of your life that God could rehabilitate, what would that part be?

Is it your emotional health?

Does it have to do with your relationships?

Does it have to do with your habits?

What part of you do you most want God to restore?

I want to encourage you to think of God as the compassionate Father He is. You have a Restorer who has great compassion for you.

God doesn't look on your brokenness with a detached sense of distance. He loves you. You are glorious to Him, even with all your flaws. He has invested in you. He has reached out to you. He sees who you will become in Christ. He is rehabilitating you. He is restoring you. He is re-creating you. He is renewing you.

I want you to imagine a life when, every time you have a setback or are discouraged, you can look in the mirror and say, "You know what, there might be some ruined parts of me, but I am a glorious ruin because of who made me. I am a new creation in Christ Jesus, and I am being restored. There is hope for me. When the people I love seem hopeless, I know there is hope for them too."

I want you to imagine a life when, every time those closest to you aren't perfect, you are able to remember they are still made in the image of God and remind yourself that God is still working on the ruined parts of them, just like He is still working on you.

I want you to imagine living in a society where every human being, regardless of their political affiliation or disabilities, is treated like a classic Ferrari. Each person is handled with inherent value, respect, and dignity. Wouldn't that be a great society to be part of? Wouldn't that obliterate the problems politicians are striving to solve?

That is the perfect society we will experience for eternity in heaven. And that's the society that God is building on earth in His church.

Better Understanding Myself and Others

Three things are true about you.

1. You are glorious because you are made in God's image,
2. You were ruined by sin, and
3. You are being restored in God's hands because of your faith in Christ.

These same three things are true of all believers.

We have about seven billion neighbors in our world today. Some are Republicans, some are Democrats, some claim to be Christians but do not live like it, some are Muslims, some are atheists. All of us have this in common: we are glorious, made in the image of our Creator. We are ruined to some extent. And our good God desires to restore all of us, if we will believe.

This is why the Scriptures tell us God desires for all people to come to salvation.[5] There's no murderer on death row, no person of any belief, no one in any disagreement with you who is not still these three things:

1. Made in the image of God.
2. Broken by sin and evil.

3. Capable of being restored by the work of Christ and the hands of almighty God.

Even the "worst of sinners" is a glorious ruin capable of restoration if they will turn to Christ. And this is why God has left us here in this broken world, so that we can declare the Good News of Jesus, so that we can bring as many "barn find" cars into God's repair shop as possible, and so that we can bring as many eternal souls into heaven as possible.

Glorious Ruins Needing Restoration

If we will see ourselves in this way, as glorious ruins needing restoration, then our lives will make more sense. If we also see the people around us in this way, then our world and its events will make more sense too.

Our failures will make sense (we are still ruined), but our failures will also not be final or fatal (we can be restored!). We'll also understand why good people (glorious) can sometimes do bad things (ruined). And we will understand why the worst of people (ruined) are capable of being redeemed (restored) in the hands of Christ.

We'll understand how other people who truly love us can so deeply wrong and harm us. And when we are wronged or harmed, we will know that every pain can be restored and repaired, if we will surrender it into the hands of the almighty Restorer.

With this view of humanity, we can better understand why the evils of war, murder, and terrorism exist. Those involved in such acts are proving how ruined the world is. They are demonstrating how desperately humanity needs the restoration Christ makes available.

***

Why does the "me" in "Jesus Loves Me" matter? Why is this a Christian essential? The answer is very simple. If humans were not ruined, then we would not need a Savior who can restore us. If we were not sinners, we would not need the cross, which is the very center and high point of Christianity.

If all people were good by nature, if people were not slaves to sin, if we did not die physically or have pain and suffering, then we would not need the gifts that Jesus provided at the cross.

But the reality, not only according to Scripture but also according to the bloodshed and genocide of human history, is that *humanity does need a Savior.* We need a perfect Hero who can not only rescue us from evil but also restore us from within. We need a perfect Restorer who can see our value and our flaws simultaneously. We need a Master Rebuilder who can sort (or sift) our dignity from our disaster.

When Jesus died as Messiah for our sins, He provided a bridge back to God. Without that bridge our bodies die, our hearts lie, and our sin natures cause us to do evil to ourselves and others.

Through Christ, we can acknowledge the God-given dignity sewn into all people. We can also see the ruined parts in ourselves. And we can live a life of positive hope that all ruined things will be restored when surrendered to our loving Creator.

As you confirm your beliefs about human nature, human need, and our human future with God, here is a prayer to help you move these beliefs from your head to your heart.

Father,

I am so thankful that when I was rusting and corroding, You didn't leave me in the junk heap of the universe. Almighty God, when humanity turned away from You, You could have discarded Planet Earth and been done with us. You could have said, "It's too much mess, too much work, too much pain."

Instead, You saw our flaws and our brokenness. Jesus, You felt our pain and experienced our consequences so You could buy us back. Lord, I belong to You. I invite You to continue restoring me. I give You the keys to my life. I give You full permission to change the parts of me that need to be restored. I surrender my thoughts and ask You to shape them. I surrender my relationships and my habits; shape them. Lord, make me what You desire me to be.

Would You stay close to me as the Restorer? Would You renew my mind, restore my soul, refresh my spirit, re-create my relationships?

Where things seem broken and hopeless, would You help me trust in Your process, trust in Your timing, and trust in Your capable hands?

Lord, I need to trust You for my own restoration—and also for the restoration of the people I care about so deeply.

Use me now in Your restoration work in this world. Use me to love the unlovable and to reach out to those who don't yet know You. Please use me to introduce others to Your loving and strong hands. I believe in You as a Redeemer, and I ask these things in the powerful name of Jesus. Amen.

9

Key Scriptures on "Me"

Every human is both glorious—and ruined. We are made in the image of God but contaminated by sin. Where evil has corrupted us, Jesus can restore us into a "new creation."

Humans are different from animals. Every human being is dignified and eternally valuable, because God created humans in His own image.

> Then God said, "Let us make mankind in our image, in our likeness, so that they may rule over the fish in the sea and the birds in the sky, over the livestock and all the wild animals, and over all the creatures that move along the ground."
> So God created mankind in his own image,
> in the image of God he created them;
> male and female he created them. (Genesis 1:26–27)

God crafted each of us with care, to be a masterpiece of His creation.

> For you created my inmost being;
> you knit me together in my mother's womb.

I praise you because I am fearfully and wonderfully made;
    your works are wonderful,
    I know that full well.
My frame was not hidden from you
    when I was made in the secret place,
    when I was woven together in the depths of the earth.
Your eyes saw my unformed body;
    all the days ordained for me were written in your book
    before one of them came to be. (Psalm 139:13–16)

And yet, while all humans are glorious, all humans are also ruined to some extent by the spiritual pollution in our world.

To be sure, *sin was in the world before the law was given*, but sin is not charged against anyone's account where there is no law. (Romans 5:13)

This pollution of sin, or evil, began when early humans chose to turn away from God, inviting evil, sin, and death into our world.

Nevertheless, death reigned *from the time of Adam* to the time of Moses. (Romans 5:14)

Because we inherit a world polluted by spiritual evil, we ourselves are spiritually polluted and cannot be transported to heaven or eternal life until we are cleaned from our spiritual pollution.

For all have sinned and fall short of the glory of God. (Romans 3:23)

We have a "sin nature" that can deceive us into making dangerous choices.

The heart is more deceitful than all else and is desperately sick; who can understand it? (Jeremiah 17:9 NASB)

When God saw us in this position, He did not walk away. He became human, in Jesus, to provide a bridge back to heaven and eternal life.

For the wages [or consequences] of sin is death, but the gift of God is eternal life in Christ Jesus our Lord. (Romans 6:23)

Restoration to God's perfect design is available to all who believe in Jesus and His work on the cross.

For if, by the trespass of the one man [Adam], death reigned through that one man, how much more will those who receive God's abundant provision of grace and of the gift of righteousness reign in life through the one man, Jesus Christ! (Romans 5:17)

We cannot earn the forgiveness of our sins or eternal life, but Jesus has already earned them. We can claim them and receive them when we believe in Jesus by faith.

For it is by grace you have been saved, through faith—and this is not from yourselves, it is the gift of God—not by works, so that no one can boast. (Ephesians 2:8–9)

Once we place our faith in Christ, we become a new creation, and God gives us a new nature that desires to live out His works and ways.

Therefore, if anyone is in Christ, the new creation has come: The old has gone, the new is here! (2 Corinthians 5:17)

PART 4

THIS I KNOW

Do I Merely Know about Jesus, or Am I Sure I Belong to God's Family? Do I Know That No Sin or Mistake Stands between God and Me? On a Scale of 1 to 10, How Sure Am I That I Will Spend Eternity in Heaven?

We cannot earn salvation by trying hard or being good enough.

For it is by grace you have been saved, through faith—and this is not from yourselves, it is the gift of God—not by works, so that no one can boast. (Ephesians 2:8–9)

We must admit our need, acknowledge Jesus as God, and believe in His work on the cross.

If you declare with your mouth, "Jesus is Lord," and believe in your heart that God raised him from the dead, you will be saved. For it is with your heart that you believe and are justified, and it is with your mouth that you profess your faith and are saved. (Romans 10:9–10)

Believing in Jesus brings the power of God into our lives, resulting in our salvation.

For I am not ashamed of the gospel, because it is the power of God that brings salvation to everyone who believes. (Romans 1:16)

Jesus says that those who do not believe in Him will not receive the gift of eternal life.

Whoever believes and is baptized will be saved, but *whoever does not believe will be condemned.* (Mark 16:16)

10

Knowing Your Salvation

Do I Merely Know about Jesus, or Am I Sure I Belong to God's Family? Do I Know That No Sin or Mistake Stands between God and Me?

The man was in tears. Our Sunday sermon described Jesus's work on the cross. Dozens of people were being baptized. That's when he came forward to talk to me.

"I've been in church for ten years," he said. "But today is the day that I'm finally believing this for myself. It's no longer what my wife believes or what the church believes. It's what I believe."

I wonder, Have you had a moment like that? Have you had a moment when you chose Jesus as your Savior, for the forgiveness of your sins? *Have you had a defining moment when you chose to believe in Christ for yourself?*

This chapter is about how simple that choice is and how important it is for you to know with certainty that you've made that choice. It's a choice only you can make. Your loved ones cannot make it for you.

To Be Saved

People who are learning about Jesus for the first time often have many questions. I'll cover a few in this section.

What must you do to be saved?

A man asked this exact question sometime after Jesus rose from the dead. The disciples answered him like this:

Believe in the Lord Jesus, and you will be saved. (Acts 16:31)

The man who asked the question learned what these words meant, just as we have been learning. He learned that the word "Lord" meant Master and God. He learned that "Jesus" was a real person who claimed to be God and had died on the cross and risen again. He even learned that "Christ" meant the Messiah.

These are the beliefs summarized in the statement "believe in the name of the Lord Jesus."

How do you become a believer in Jesus—a Christian?

The answer can be found in the Word of God.

If you declare with your mouth, "Jesus is Lord," and believe in your heart that God raised him from the dead, you will be saved. For it is with your heart that you believe and are justified, and it is with your mouth that you profess your faith and are saved. (Romans 10:9–10)

You can know with certainty that you have received God's gift of salvation, His forgiveness of your sins, and eternal life.

God's Word is clear that you can know today and every day that your sins are forgiven. You can know with certainty that your soul has been made right with God. This does not happen as the result of "good works" you perform or achieve. Instead, you must have a moment when you choose to submit to God, believe in Jesus's work on the cross, and receive His gift of salvation.

What does it mean to repent?

We must repent—that is, turn away from self-dependence and sin and believe in Jesus—to receive God's free gift of salvation.

> For it is by grace you have been saved, through faith—and this is not from yourselves, it is the gift of God—not by works, so that no one can boast. (Ephesians 2:8–9)

Remember the man who came up to me in tears on that Sunday morning? He had been in church for ten years and had heard many sermons and facts about Jesus. He had even mentally agreed that these facts were correct. But he had never before chosen at the heart level to call out to God for the salvation of his own soul. On that day he "humbled himself" before God and admitted his need, while choosing to believe.

In the same way, it is possible for you to intellectually know all the correct facts about Christianity, and yet not personally believe in a way that applies this power to your heart and soul.

Scripture states that, "even the demons believe this, and they tremble in terror" (James 2:19). That is, the demons have the correct facts about Jesus and what He did on the cross, but they have not submitted to Jesus as their Lord, their Master, their Boss. They have not asked Him to forgive their sins.

This chapter provides a great time for you—or anyone in your reading group—to ensure that you have had a personal moment of willing surrender to Jesus, in which you admit your need for His forgiveness and rescue. Today is the day to ensure you have personally called out to Him in this way, believing in His work on the cross. This includes the heart submission that you choose to make Jesus your Lord, your Master, your Boss. When you do this as an act of faith from your heart, you receive God's free gift of salvation.

The Bridge

As we go over these next few questions, think back to the image we discussed in part 2 of Jesus's work on the cross creating a bridge between God and humanity.

Is anything separating you from God?

We've learned that "all have sinned and fall short of the glory of God" (Romans 3:23). Our sin separates us from God. This is why we need the work of Jesus on the cross.[1] At the cross Jesus paid the penalty for our mistakes.[2] At the cross Jesus took the just punishment and consequence for my sins and yours.[3]

The original sin of Adam and Eve has spread to all of humanity, separating every person from the eternal life of God. When our sin separates us from God, we are detached from the joy of being in relationship with Him. We are detached from the eternal life that God provides as the source of life. We are detached from the victory over sin and shame that is found in Christ.

Only when our sin is covered do we become fully reconnected to God. And fully covering our sin is precisely the work that Jesus did on the cross.

Have you ever stood at the edge of a large chasm or canyon?

Remember the Grand Canyon divide we talked about in chapter 5? When you stand at the edge of the Grand Canyon, you can see the cliff at your feet going straight down for the distance of a mile. Then, when you look out, you see a void, a chasm, a gap that is far across. On the other side of the canyon is a similar cliff that climbs back up to the same height. It is a massive divide from one side to the other.

Now imagine yourself standing on one edge of this massive canyon, at the very top of the cliff. Visualize God all the way over on the other side—far, far away.

The Word of God says that our sins have separated us from God in this exact way. Remember, if we picture it like this, then Jesus's work on the cross is like a bridge that He built between the two sides. Anyone who chooses to believe in Jesus steps onto this bridge, to be reconnected with God.

Let's look once again at the bridge Jesus created when He died on the cross.

GOD'S RESCUE

GOD

THE CHRIST

DEATH
ANXIETY
BROKEN
RELATIONSHIPS

ETERNAL LIFE
PEACE
RESTORED
RELATIONSHIPS

Aaron Williams

"For the **wages** of sin is **death**, but the **gift** of God is **eternal life** through **Christ Jesus** our Lord."

ROMANS 6:23

Where do you find yourself today in this picture?

Have you had a moment when you've set foot by faith onto the bridge of the cross by believing in Christ for yourself?

Do you know with certainty that all your sins—past, present, and future—have been forgiven?

Do you know with certainty that you have eternal life, that you will be with God in heaven after your last breath on earth?

Take a moment right now and think. Where are you on that visual?

The gift of God is eternal life through Jesus Christ our Lord. One of the hardest things about receiving a gift is that you cannot take any credit for it. I have met people who hear this offer of salvation through Jesus and respond, "It's just too easy. It can't possibly be that easy."

Well, here's what is not easy about it: you have to admit you cannot fix this sin problem in your own strength.

You have to admit you can't jump your way across the chasm to God. When people try to earn or work their way to God, they fall into the trap of religion, which is thinking that we can do enough good deeds to cross the chasm. Scripture is clear that only Jesus was good enough to bridge the divide.

You set foot onto the bridge of salvation with a heart that says, "God, I acknowledge that I cannot fix myself. I cannot forgive my sin. I cannot earn eternal life. I cannot fix what is broken inside me, but Jesus, I believe that You can."

Jesus once said that it's easier for a camel—a big, tall camel—to kneel down and go through the eye of a needle than it is for a rich person to enter the kingdom of God.[4]

Why did Jesus say that?

Jesus's statement wasn't primarily about money. It was about pride. People who think they can solve all their problems without God's help will not be in the kingdom of God, according to Jesus. Scripture actually declares, "God is opposed to the proud, but gives grace to the humble. Therefore humble yourselves under the mighty hand of God" (1 Peter 5:5–6 NASB).

You can have $0 in the bank and still have a prideful heart that prohibits you from stepping onto the bridge of salvation. Pride is nothing more than an unhealthy self-dependence that says, "I don't need God."

When Jesus said it's easier for a camel to go through a tiny eyelet of a needle than a rich person to enter God's kingdom, he was talking about our self-dependent pride. He was describing the reality that our "ruined" sin nature refuses to humble itself before God and refuses to acknowledge when we need God's help.

God is eager to give us a new nature, if we will humble ourselves and call out for His help.

How do you step onto God's bridge of salvation and receive this gift?

God tells you exactly how to receive His gift of salvation in Romans 10:9–10.

> If you declare with your mouth, "Jesus is Lord," and believe in your heart that God raised him from the dead, you will be saved. For it is with your heart that you believe and are justified, and it is with your mouth that you profess your faith and are saved.

Here is a prayer to move these truths from your head to your heart, from facts you know to faith you choose. The words of this prayer are not magical, but the ideas in this prayer hold all the power of the universe, if you pray them from the heart in faith to your Creator.

Dear Jesus,

I come to You, the almighty God, and I acknowledge that my life falls short. I have sinned and wronged You in many ways. Jesus, I thank You for dying on the cross for my sins and mistakes. Today I acknowledge You as Lord and Leader of my life. I repent and turn away from my pride. I believe in You with my heart, and I choose to follow You with my life. I want to receive Your free gift of salvation.

Jesus, through Your work on the cross, please forgive my sins. Please adopt me into the family of God. Please give me a new nature and a new identity.

Thank You for loving me. Thank You for choosing me. Thank You for laying down Your life so that I can have eternal life with You in heaven.

*Lord, help me live as a new creation now. Help me serve
You all my days. I pray this in Your name and believing in
Your work, Jesus. Amen.*

If you're praying this for the first time, please let me know so I can celebrate with you. You can shoot me an email at John.Dickerson@ ConnectionPointe.org or tell me on social media @JohnSDickerson.

What Happens Next?

After you believe in Jesus, you are adopted into the family of God, and God gives you thousands of promises. Here is one promise about your new identity.

> For those who are led by the Spirit of God are the children of God.
> The Spirit you received does not make you slaves, so that you live
> in fear again; rather, the Spirit you received brought about your
> adoption to sonship. And by him we cry, "Abba, Father." The Spirit
> himself testifies with our spirit that we are God's children. Now
> if we are children, then we are heirs—heirs of God and co-heirs
> with Christ, if indeed we share in his sufferings in order that we
> may also share in his glory. (Romans 8:14–17)

Jesus says your next step, after you believe and repent, is to publicly declare your faith by being baptized. You may recall the final words of Jesus to His disciples when He told them: "Go and make disciples . . . baptizing them" (Matthew 28:19).

Water baptism is the moment when you "go public" with your faith, much like a wedding is the moment when two people formalize their love publicly. As Romans 10:10 states, your belief begins in your heart, and then "with your mouth . . . you profess your faith."

Our salvation is not earned by baptism or any other work we can perform. We are saved solely by Jesus's work on the cross. Jesus tells all who believe in Him to be baptized as a demonstration of faith in His work on the cross.

Whoever believes and is baptized will be saved, but whoever does not believe will be condemned. (Mark 16:16)

As Jesus's first disciples began spreading the Good News of salvation, it was the norm for new believers to express their faith in Him by being baptized, just as Jesus had commanded in Matthew 28. One example of this is recorded in Acts 2.

After Peter preached about Jesus being the Messiah, some three thousand people believed. Peter ends his sermon about Jesus by saying, "God has made this Jesus, whom you crucified, both Lord and Messiah" (Acts 2:36).

Now, here's how the people responded and how Peter instructed them to become followers of Jesus:

When the people heard this [Peter's sermon that Jesus is the Messiah], they were cut to the heart and said to Peter and the other apostles, "Brothers, what shall we do?"

Peter replied, "Repent and be baptized, every one of you, in the name of Jesus Christ for the forgiveness of your sins. And you will receive the gift of the Holy Spirit. The promise is for you and your children and for all who are far off—for all whom the Lord our God will call." (Acts 2:37–39)

If you've never been baptized by another believer, Jesus says to do so. If you don't yet have a church home, my church family would be thrilled to baptize you as a believer in Christ. We likely have someone in our movement who lives near you. Or you could travel to Indianapolis to be baptized, as many of our church's online viewers have done.

Visit www.ConnectionPointe.org, and we can talk with you to get you scheduled to be baptized.

And did you notice in the passage above that you "receive the gift of the Holy Spirit" after you believe? We will explore this powerful presence of God in your life in part 6.

11

Pictures of Your Salvation

On a Scale of 1 to 10, How Sure Am I That I Will Spend Eternity in Heaven?

Let's savor the significance of our faith in Christ with three true stories.

The first helps us appreciate what Jesus did by coming to earth.

The second helps us appreciate the importance of our response to Him.

The third helps us be secure as His adopted children, confident in Him because of His unchanging love.

One: Leaving Heaven to Rescue Earth

In August 2010, a collapsed mineshaft trapped thirty-three miners deep underground.[1] You may remember this worldwide news story. A gold mine in the country of Chile collapsed, trapping the miners deep below the earth.

For about two weeks, the whole world thought these miners were dead. Then someone figured out that these guys, these thirty-three miners, were alive at the bottom of this mineshaft. They were stuck in the rubble. Trapped in the darkness with little water and no food, the miners were days away from death.

What followed was one of the greatest rescue missions in human history. Nations from all around the world gathered. NASA sent top engineers to help the Chilean government figure out how they could possibly drill down through the rock to rescue these guys who were buried so deep underground.

In a diagram showing the collapsed mineshaft from the side, the whole underground mine looked like a tilting Jenga tower. When the experts attempted to drill down through the rubble to reach the trapped miners, they kept failing. The rock between the miners and the people was just too thick.

Then, on the third attempt, drilling through solid rock, they finally cut a small channel into a chamber, a cavity in the earth from which the miners could be rescued.

Here's what I love about this picture: this is exactly how God describes humanity right now. He actually says we are born into a world that is collapsed and trapped in sin.[2] We are born into a world that has fallen in on itself.

Because we are made in the image of God, we still have remarkable capacity in this fallen world. We marvel at human inventions and innovations. But ultimately, for all our human progress, our bodies still die. Nations still war against nations. Terrorists still kill innocent people. Jails, prisons, and courts are still needed because even educated people still commit crimes against each other.

Humanity is like those trapped miners; our lifespan of about eighty or ninety years is like the rock ceiling above our heads. No matter how many toys we gather around ourselves, we are powerless to break out into eternal life.

When Jesus came down into this world, He cut through the thick rock layers of the universe and drilled down into our collapsed world. The God who created everything gave His life to create an escape tunnel. He made a way out.

Jesus often told humans who were arguing about politics or money, "My kingdom is not of this world" (John 18:36). Jesus was saying, more or less, "You guys are arguing about who is in charge of the food rations or who gets to sit on a throne in this collapsed mineshaft. You're arguing about who owns the most land or has the most influence here in a dark and dirty place. Go ahead, argue away. I came to drill a tunnel out of this mess, into a higher realm, a higher kingdom. I came to set people completely free from the darkness and the death and the dustiness of this collapsed world."[3]

From August to October 2010, for sixty-nine days, those thirty-three miners lived in the darkness, knowing that rescue was coming from above. Through that first small channel that had been drilled down, the rescuers began sending food and messages, very much like how God sent prophets and revelations leading up to Jesus's time on earth. Finally, the miners' rescue did arrive, in the form of a giant metal capsule called the Phoenix.

Each miner had to step inside of this Phoenix capsule. The rescue capsule could only carry one person up at a time—but it could keep operating for every miner who chose to step into it and be rescued.

It's a fitting image of our salvation, provided through Christ, because this is exactly how it works with God. He has done the hard work. He has made the self-sacrifice to drill down into our lives. He has provided the path to salvation, but each individual person must choose to believe and step into His rescue.

This Phoenix rescue capsule was lowered through a tunnel of rock to thump down at the bottom of the mineshaft, deep underground. Each miner then had to decide for themselves, *Will I step into this thing?*

It surely felt claustrophobic. Some may have even wondered, *Will I get strapped into this thing and be lifted up by a winch— held only by a wire rope in a super-long tunnel that goes straight down? If that rope breaks, I'm dead. Am I going to trust in that? Am I going to put my faith in that?*

By placing their faith in the rescue vehicle, each miner was acknowledging that they could not rescue themselves. They could not dig their own way out of the rubble. In this same way, we cannot dig our way to heaven, to immortality, or to a life free from sin and shame.

As we talked about earlier, Jesus claimed to be the only way out of the rubble and brokenness of this world. There are not multiple paths that lead to heaven, according to Jesus. He put it this way: "I am the way and the truth and the life. No one comes to the Father except through me" (John 14:6).

God's only way out is narrow, but the Way is open to all. God desires for all people to come to that salvation. He desires that everyone would choose to believe.[4]

Two: The Importance of Your Response to Jesus

When I was working as a newspaper reporter and journalist, my editor assigned me to write a story about a heroin drug epidemic that was spreading in Phoenix, Arizona. To show the sad and deadly end of heroin, I profiled a twenty-one-year-old addict named Mickey.[5]

Mickey had grown up in a good, middle-upper-class family. Her dad was an attorney, and she had an ideal childhood. But somewhere along the way, a friend gave Mickey some heroin. She injected some in her arm, and from that day on, she was an addict.

When I met Mickey, she had been addicted to heroin for about two years. She was down to eighty-five or ninety pounds, and the heroin use was devouring her body. She was just this skinny, little, shaking creature with electric blue eyes.

For my profile, I would meet Mickey at the drug house where she lived. We would walk together to a Jack-in-the-Box restaurant in the neighborhood. We would sit in a booth, and I would ask Mickey about life as a heroin addict. She would describe her life with these traumatic sentences. She would blur words together like "agonizing" and "anguishing," creating words like "agishing." Her brain was just so messed up from the drugs.

Mickey was at a point where she knew she was dying from her addiction. She had seen other heroin addicts die at her drug house. She wanted to get free from the addiction and lifestyle.

As I was meeting with Mickey, I was also talking with the best addiction recovery center in the state of Arizona. I pitched an idea to the recovery center. I said, "Hey, I know six months of treatment costs tens of thousands of dollars, but what if Mickey agreed to do the treatment? I could write about the treatment process. We would publish the stories, and it would be a lot of great publicity for you guys. Would you give Mickey treatment for free if I agreed to write stories about the process?"

They said yes, and I talked to Mickey about the treatment. She said she wanted the help. She wanted to change.

So, we got it all set up. The day was scheduled where we would pull up in a vehicle in front of the drug house where Mickey lived.

Mickey didn't have to pay anything. She didn't have to earn this live-saving treatment. She didn't have to achieve it. But to receive the help she would have to walk out the front door of that drug house. Using her own free will, she would have to choose to walk down twenty feet of sidewalk and get into the vehicle headed for the treatment facility.

The scheduled day arrived, and the van from the treatment center pulled up in front of the house, waiting for Mickey. I sat there watching the front door. Five minutes turned into ten. Soon it had been fifteen minutes, and then twenty.

I finally went and knocked on the front door.

"Is Mickey here?"

"Yeah, Mickey is here."

She and I had a conversation that day, and she told me she did not have the willpower to move herself outside. She would not get into the vehicle that could rescue her and save her life.

My entire arrangement with the treatment center was built on the agreement that people cannot go into drug treatment unless they want to be treated. The center had been at this long enough to know that the treatment doesn't work if the addict does not desire to be set free.

Mickey had a free gift offered to her. She was in a life-or-death situation. And in the moment, she just would not choose to receive the gift.

I wonder if you would pause for a moment to answer this question thoughtfully: *Do you know for sure that you have received the free gift of God's salvation?*

Receiving His gift is as simple as declaring with your mouth that Jesus is Lord and believing in your heart that God raised Him from the dead.

God desires for you to be sure of your salvation and your right relationship with Him. You can do better than *hoping* that if you die, you *might* be with God in heaven. You can know for sure that heaven is your home, your future, and your hope.

You get this certainty when you receive God's free offer of salvation.

I wonder, on a scale of 1 to 10, with 10 being "I know for sure that my last breath on earth will be followed by my first breath in heaven. I'm absolutely confident of it," at what number would you place your certainty that you will spend eternity with God in heaven?

Are you a 7? A 6? An 8.5? God desires for you to live every day with a 10-out-of-10 certainty of your eternal destination, sealed and assured through the work of Christ on the cross.

If you don't know your eternal salvation as a 10-out-of-10 certainty, today can be the day you assure yourself of that. Today can be a day you can look back on for the rest of your life—and you can grow in love with God the rest of your life.

The moment you believe in Jesus (as described in the previous chapter), something supernatural happens in your soul, in your life, and in your eternity. God breaks the chains of sin off you. He creates a place for you in His home and adopts you into His family.

There is now nothing you can do to outrun the love that God has for you in Christ Jesus.[6] God is your Father, and He loves you. You also have a spiritual family of other believers to journey with you and encourage you on the road to heaven.

Three: Living as God's Children

Did you know that you are an heir to the largest fortune in human history?

That's right. As a believer in Christ, adopted into the family of God, all of Christ's possessions become yours. I'm not the one making this claim. God promises you in Romans 8 that you are a "co-heir" with Christ in the kingdom He is building and preparing.

You can be confident that your sins are forgiven. You can be confident about the inheritance that awaits you. As a child of God, you now have a stability, a confidence, and an identity that can carry you through any failure or difficulty in this world.

Parenting my three young children gives me momentary glimpses of how God the Father must see us. Like all kids, my children do some silly things. Sometimes they even do stupid things, but I never stop loving them.

In fact, when one was a toddler, that child would sometimes say, "I don't love you anymore," or "I don't want to play with you ever again." Those impulsive moments and words never stopped me from loving them. And our impulsive failures cannot stop our Father from loving us.

When my children are tired, hungry, excited, happy, or one hundred other emotions, I get to see what God the Father's view of us must be. After all, we are His children in Christ.

One day, when one of my children was finishing up with potty training, I got to experience how God's love enters into our yuckiness, into the mess of our lives.

I walked into my child's bedroom, and this child was sitting on the floor, changing their clothes. It's normal for a child to have a lot of "accidents" during those first weeks of potty training. They've been used to wearing pull-up diapers, and now they are learning to function in normal underwear.

It was in this context that I looked down at the bedroom rug and saw a little pyramid of toilet paper and baby diaper wipes that appeared to be covering something.

"What's that?" I asked, pointing down to the pyramid that was clearly covering up some kind of accident.

My child said, "That's nothing, Daddy." Then, looking ashamed, my child said, "Can you please leave?"

I sensed embarrassment. And while I was pretty sure there was soiled underwear sitting on the rug, I tried to play it cool. It was one of those parenting moments when I was thinking, *Okay, fragile little ego, learning moment, important moment, how do I handle this?*

So I walked out into the hall and thought for a moment.

I remember thinking, *I don't want to shame my child and give them a complex about going to the bathroom.*

I formulated a plan and walked back into the room.

"Hey, first of all, I want you to know that you are really doing a good job with the potty training," I told my child.

"And also, it's normal to have some accidents while you are still getting this figured out. I just want you to know that if there *is* something under that toilet paper . . . if there is something under there, well, do you maybe feel embarrassed that there might be something under there?"

My child nodded.

"If you feel a little embarrassed, here's what I want you to know. Your mom and I love you, and any time you feel that embarrassed feeling, you need to know we are here to help you."

Now, I have this quirk as a parent. As soon as my children can mumble words, I begin telling them grown-up ideas. I continued talking to this preschool-aged child.

"What you're feeling, people call it shame or embarrassment. And whenever you feel those feelings, you don't have to run away or hide. You can run to us, and we will always help you. We are here to help you clean up your messes, and we are here to help you learn."

I have no idea how much of that interaction my child remembers now. But I ended up learning something in the process. After I cleaned up the mess that was indeed hiding under the toilet paper, and my child was dressed in clean warm clothes and comfortably playing near me, I realized something.

I realized that every time I feel ashamed or embarrassed about my mistakes or failures, my Father in heaven feels the same way about me as I did about my child.

As children of God, why is it that some days we don't feel God's love for us? In my experience it's usually because we have things in our lives that we are embarrassed about.

We have things in our lives that we are ashamed of. We have guilt, or we have shame, and whether we have the words for it or not, we assume God wouldn't want to be near us in our mess. We feel there is something between us and God.

When Jesus came to earth, what He did on the cross is this: He willingly laid down His life to do the cleanup. God promises, "If we confess our sins, He is faithful and righteous to forgive us our sins and to cleanse us from all unrighteousness" (1 John 1:9 NASB).

At the cross, Jesus took upon Himself every shameful and embarrassing thing we've ever done. He took our evil upon Himself. Every murder that's ever been committed. Every moment of rage and hatred. All the little white lies, stolen convenience store candy bars, broken promises, and hateful thoughts.

Jesus said, essentially, "I willingly take upon myself the cleanup duty. I take the consequences for your shameful things, so that all who desire to be made right with God can receive a free gift and be restored to God."

This is what it means that God loves you.

The moment you believe in Jesus for the forgiveness of your sins, God says you are adopted into His family. Now, almighty God sees you like I saw that potty-training child with the accident on the rug. That is, He loves you no matter what mistakes you make.

As a child of God, you no longer need to live under shame or guilt. Your Creator desires to help you any time you feel those emotions. He has paid the price to wash your sins away.

As a result, "Therefore, there is now no condemnation for those who are in Christ Jesus" (Romans 8:1).

Here is a prayer of thanksgiving to help you claim your identity as a child of God.

Dear Jesus,

I thank You that when I was trapped under the weight of sin, You came down to earth on a rescue mission. Thank You for setting me free from my past, from my mistakes, from all that is broken in this world.

Oh Savior, will You help me to live today knowing that my destiny is in heaven and my identity is in You?

Because of You, I am now adopted into the very family of God. I've chosen to receive Your free gift of salvation, and now I choose to live as the coheir that I am in Your kingdom.

Father God, I pray that my new identity, my true identity, would reshape the way I think and the way I live. Help me to walk worthy of the calling You have given me. Help me live free from shame. Help me claim the fullness of life and the freedom of life that You desire for me.

Thank You for loving me enough to choose me, to adopt me, to pay the price for me, to always forgive me. Please walk with me now, and teach me to walk with You all my days. Amen.

12

Key Scriptures on "This I Know"

We cannot earn salvation, but we must use our will to admit our need (repent), acknowledge Jesus as God, and believe in His work on the cross. After we receive salvation by faith, we express that belief in Jesus through baptism.

Believing in Jesus as Savior includes a choice to turn away from our old way of thinking. The Bible uses the word "repent" to describe this moment. God desires for all people to "come to repentance," but each individual much choose for themselves if they will believe and repent.

> The Lord is not slow in keeping his promise. . . . Instead he is patient with you, not wanting anyone to perish, but everyone to come to repentance. (2 Peter 3:9)

We can know with certainty we have received God's gift of salvation, forgiveness, and eternal life. Nobody else can make this choice for us.

> If you declare with your mouth, "Jesus is Lord," and believe in your heart that God raised him from the dead, you will be saved. For it is with your heart that you believe and are justified, and it is with your mouth that you profess your faith and are saved. (Romans 10:9–10)

We cannot earn our salvation by performing any good works, and it is equally true that we must repent (turn away from our wrongdoings or sins) and believe in Jesus personally to accept or receive God's free gift of salvation.

> For it is by grace you have been saved, through faith—and this is not from yourselves, it is the gift of God—not by works, so that no one can boast. (Ephesians 2:8–9)

Believing in Jesus brings the power of God into our lives, resulting in our salvation.

> For I am not ashamed of the gospel, because it is the power of God that brings salvation to everyone who believes. (Romans 1:16)

> [Note: the word gospel here means "Good News" and refers to the good news that Jesus is God and offers a right relationship with God to all who believe.]

Jesus links our external water baptism with our internal belief. Our salvation is not earned by baptism or any other work we can do, but Jesus tells all who believe in Him to be baptized as a demonstration of their faith. If we've never been baptized, Jesus says to do so.

> Whoever believes and is baptized will be saved, but whoever does not believe will be condemned. (Mark 16:16)

After we believe in Jesus, we are empowered to live a new kind of life, as Jesus did.

> In the same way, count yourselves dead to sin but alive to God in Christ Jesus. Therefore do not let sin reign in your mortal body so

that you obey its evil desires. Do not offer any part of yourself to sin as an instrument of wickedness, but rather offer yourselves to God as those who have been brought from death to life; and offer every part of yourself to him as an instrument of righteousness. For sin shall no longer be your master, because you are not under the law, but under grace. (Romans 6:11–14)

Once we believe in Jesus, our sins are forgiven: past, present, and future. We no longer live under shame.

Therefore, there is now no condemnation for those who are in Christ Jesus. (Romans 8:1)

After we believe in Jesus, we are adopted into the very family of God.

For those who are led by the Spirit of God are the children of God. The Spirit you received does not make you slaves, so that you live in fear again; rather, the Spirit you received brought about your adoption to sonship. And by him we cry, "Abba, Father." The Spirit himself testifies with our spirit that we are God's children. Now if we are children, then we are heirs—heirs of God and co-heirs with Christ, if indeed we share in his sufferings in order that we may also share in his glory. (Romans 8:14–17)

PART 5

FOR THE BIBLE TELLS ME SO

What Does the Bible Mean for Me as a Follower of Jesus? Do I Really Need to Believe the Bible to Live in God's Power?

> **SECTION SUMMARY: We choose the Bible as the unchanging standard for all we do and believe because Jesus did. We must read and obey the Word of God to realize our identity in Christ.**

Jesus said that the Scriptures come directly from the mouth of God.

Jesus answered, "It is written: 'Man shall not live on bread alone, but on every word that comes from the mouth of God.'" (Matthew 4:4)

Jesus claimed that every word of Scripture is fixed in the universe—more so than the very planet we walk upon.

It is easier for heaven and earth to disappear than for the least stroke of a pen to drop out of the Law. (Luke 16:17)

Jesus is looking for followers who will take the Word of God seriously and teach others to do the same.

Therefore anyone who sets aside one of the least of these commands and teaches others accordingly will be called least in the kingdom of heaven, but whoever practices and teaches these commands will be called great in the kingdom of heaven. (Matthew 5:19)

All of the Bible has been breathed by God, for our benefit, to equip us in serving Him.

All Scripture is God-breathed and is useful for teaching, rebuking, correcting and training in righteousness, so that the servant of God may be thoroughly equipped for every good work. (2 Timothy 3:16–17)

The Word of God provides us with endurance, encouragement, and hope as we follow Jesus in a world that is broken.

For everything that was written in the past was written to teach us, so that through the endurance taught in the Scriptures and the encouragement they provide we might have hope. (Romans 15:4)

The words of God in the Bible are without error.

> And the words of the LORD are flawless,
>> like silver purified in a crucible,
>> like gold refined seven times. (Psalm 12:6)

13

Jesus's Standard for What You Believe

What Does the Bible Mean for Me as a Follower of Jesus?

Life isn't easy. Live long enough, and we will find ourselves in a storm of life, battling something like sickness, depression, or injustice.

When these storms come, and we face difficulty or change, how can we remain unshaken and stable and consistently follow Jesus?

God knew we would face difficulties in a broken world. And so, when Jesus lived as our example, He began His ministry with a time of demanding testing and temptation. Jesus stayed faithful to God the Father in the wilderness, where He was physically alone, hungry, and fatigued.

Jesus's wilderness is a great picture for us when we find ourselves in a wilderness of our own.

When Jesus was at His physical and emotional lowest—alone, hungry, weary, and fatigued—Satan came to Him and tempted Him to stop trusting God the Father. Just like Satan tempts us, he tempted Jesus to settle for a smaller plan than God's best.

In the wilderness, the same evil voice that whispered doubts in the ears of Adam and Eve whispered doubts in Jesus's ears. Unlike Adam and Eve, however, Jesus stood strong through the temptation. He was tempted like we are, but He never sinned.[1] Jesus's example shows us how we also can stand strong in any wilderness, storm, trial, or temptation. In Jesus's response to Satan, we learn how we should respond when Satan whispers doubts or disobedient thoughts in our ears.

So, how did Jesus respond in the wilderness? He responded by looking to Scripture as the standard for what He would do and believe.

For every temptation Satan presented to Jesus, Jesus replied with a specific Scripture. In Jesus's example, we find the source of stability that we need to follow God now.

1. Jesus said that the Scriptures come directly from the mouth of God.

   > Jesus answered, "It is written: 'Man shall not live on bread alone, but on every word that *comes from the mouth of God*.'" (Matthew 4:4)

2. Jesus referred to Scripture as His standard for truth and authority.

   > Jesus said to him, ". . . *For it is written*, 'Worship the Lord your God, and serve him only.'" (Matthew 4:10)

3. Jesus modeled that the Scriptures provide power to avoid deadly temptation. He claimed that humans can and

should feed on the Word of God as eagerly as we feed on physical food.

> Jesus answered, "It is written: '*Man shall not live on bread alone*, but on every word that comes from the mouth of God.'" (Matthew 4:4)

Both verses above come from Jesus's trials in the wilderness. He leaned on Scripture as His truth and source of strength in His response to each of Satan's three temptations. This dependence on Scripture is a model for us as we seek to obey God and live a life of freedom.

God's Word Is the Standard

To fully experience our new identity in Christ, we choose to make God's Word the standard for all we do and believe. The Bible expresses the very heart of God. As such, we cannot claim to love and follow Jesus without treasuring His words. Because Jesus made Scripture His standard for all He did and believed, we do the same.

We've seen from Jesus's example that Scripture stabilizes us in an unstable world. It is our source of strength and truth, helping us be fruitful and flourish in a world that is chaotic, unpredictable, and always changing.

In 2 Timothy 3, God uses a letter from Paul the Apostle to prepare us for facing difficulties in this world that is broken by sin. For some believers, the entire culture and society around us will shake. Other times, we may face spiritual attack. Still other times, our own lives and worlds will shake with difficulty. Bad days will happen. There will be times when people lose their perspective. There will be times when people lose their morality. There will even be times when people lose their sanity. Here's how God's Word describes it:

> But mark this: There will be terrible times in the last days. People will be lovers of themselves, lovers of money, boastful, proud, abusive,

disobedient to their parents, ungrateful, unholy, without love, un-
forgiving, slanderous, without self-control. (2 Timothy 3:1–3)

These harmful people will slander others. They will live without
self-control. We can see such people causing upheaval and pain.
In most societies those are often instigated by those who behave
as Paul is describing here. The list continues. Let's keep reading.
These people are

brutal, not lovers of the good, treacherous, rash, conceited, lovers
of pleasure rather than lovers of God—having a form of godliness
but denying its power. (2 Timothy 3:3–5)

Because they do not have the power of God in their lives, these
people will be conceited. They will be lovers of pleasure, rather
than lovers of God. They will have "a form of godliness," meaning
they might even claim to be Christians. They might claim to be
followers of Jesus but do not actually have the power of God—
because they have not plugged into Jesus's beliefs.

Paul continues to say that even within churches and spiritual
communities, sometimes there will be false teachers or spiritual
leaders who drift away from God. These false teachers will be
"evildoers and imposters [who] will go from bad to worse, deceiving and being deceived" (2 Timothy 3:13).

These false teachers, who claim to be representatives of God,
will only get worse over time. They will deceive many, leading
vulnerable people away from God's truth and help. Apparently,
they themselves will be deceived, and so they might even think
that what they're doing is noble or good.

This chapter of God's Word definitely paints a picture of a
difficult environment. But there is hope.

*What will keep us connected to Jesus at a time when many
people and even some "churches" and "pastors" abandon Jesus's
true teaching?* Here's how we can stay true to Jesus, according to
the Word of God:

> But as for you, continue in what you have learned and have become convinced of, because you know those from whom you learned it, and how from infancy *you have known the Holy Scriptures, which are able to make you wise for salvation through faith in Christ Jesus.* (2 Timothy 3:14–15)

We can find stability in knowing "the Holy Scriptures," another term for the Bible or Word of God. We can be unshaken in the midst of a shaking world when we "continue in what [we] have learned." That is, continue in the essential beliefs of Christianity. We must hold tight to them and keep building on them, never allowing Satan to convince us to abandon these essentials.

God's Word is our anchor. We should cling to His Word no matter what anyone around us does or says, for "the Holy Scriptures . . . are able to make [us] wise for salvation through faith in Christ Jesus."

God is teaching us to cling to His unchanging Word, no matter what anyone around us does or says. Paul the Apostle wrote these words to Timothy, a young Jesus follower, at the end of his fruitful ministry and life. In the letter Paul was saying, "I'm about done." He knew he was about to die, about to move upward to heaven. Paul warned Timothy, saying in essence, "Some crazy things will happen in your life." And this is true in our lives too.

Until Christ returns, the "ruined" part of human nature will continue to undermine human progress. So, Christians, no matter what happens around you, continue in what you have learned and what you have become convinced of.

God gives us this promise: Scripture will stabilize us in a shaking world.

All Scripture Is God-Breathed

According to God, our Christian Bible is "breathed" by Him. The same Creator who breathed life into existence (see Genesis 1), breathed a battery—a reservoir of supernatural life—into the words and ideas of the Christian Bible. We can draw life and stability out of these words at any time, any day. And this is for our benefit, to equip us in serving Him.

> All Scripture is God-breathed and is useful for teaching, rebuking, correcting and training in righteousness, so that the servant of God may be thoroughly equipped for every good work. (2 Timothy 3:16–17)

All Scripture is useful. It's profitable for teaching, not just generically, but for teaching our souls how to live in the specific circumstances of our lives. The Word of God also corrects us. It trains us in right living. It stabilizes and strengthens you and me to live the good lives God has prepared for us as followers of Christ.

This might seem like a strange idea, that a big old book has the power to stabilize our lives in any challenge or circumstance. But when we refer to the Bible, we're not talking about any old book. Yes, the Bible is, technically, old. But the Bible is not a book of myths. The cities and characters the Bible mentions all existed. The Bible is historically valid, and yet it's so much more than a history book.

God gave you the Bible to feed you in every season of life. As a follower of Christ, you cannot find the fullness of what God has for you in life apart from His words in Scripture. This is the final prong of our Christian essentials: "Jesus / loves / me / This I know / **for the Bible tells me so.**"

Since Jesus relied on Scripture to live a sinless life, then you and I surely need Scripture to live the lives God has planned for us. We must learn to highly value this final prong on our power plug, the Bible.

This essential belief can be summarized like this: *If I want to grow as a Christian, if I really want to see God's power change my thinking and make me a new person, then I must submit to and treasure the Bible as God's very words to me.*

If I will look to the Bible as the authority for what I decide to do in my life and what I decide to believe, then the Bible will keep me in God's restoring hands. It will keep me in a place where He can keep working on me.

In part 3 of this book we talked about "me." We learned that we are glorious ruins, like rusted classic cars. The moment we trust in Christ, God begins restoring us. It's a lifelong process. Until we get to heaven, we are in God's repair shop. And the Word of God is a primary tool God uses to rebuild us, so we can live and function as "new creations."

God's Word Is Loved by Many

The same Scriptures that lead us to salvation are trustworthy in all other matters.

> For everything that was written in the past was written to teach us, so that through the endurance taught in the Scriptures and the encouragement they provide we might have hope. (Romans 15:4)

The words of God in the Bible are without error in all that they teach us.

> And the words of the LORD are flawless,
> like silver purified in a crucible,
> like gold refined seven times. (Psalm 12:6)

Jesus claimed that every word of Scripture is fixed in the universe—more so than the very planet we walk upon.

> It is easier for heaven and earth to disappear than for the least stroke of a pen to drop out of the Law. (Luke 16:17)

We live at a time when even some followers of Jesus act embarrassed about the Bible. Outsiders may even mock us for taking the Bible seriously. When we encounter such people, we do well to remember that many rulers and cultures throughout history have also downplayed, mocked, and scorned the Bible. Those cultures and rulers have all died. And the people who mock the Bible today will also pass away and not experience eternal life.

Meanwhile, the Word of God continues to be the most influential book in the history of the world, loved by hundreds of millions more people in every subsequent generation. The Word of God will last forever.

Some of the most brilliant people in history have loved the Bible and believed it to be the very Word of God. This group includes Christians like Reverend Martin Luther King Jr., Frederick Douglass, Harriet Tubman, Isaac Newton, Blaise Pascal, Johannes Kepler, and many others. Edward Jenner, the scientist who discovered the smallpox vaccine that has now saved hundreds of millions of lives, also loved the Word of God.[2]

If anyone ever mocks you for believing the Bible to be the Word of God, remind yourself that Jesus was also mocked in His lifetime. Just like Jesus was tested in the wilderness, when you are tested you can also stand strong by remaining true to the Word of God.

You are not alone; you stand intellectually with millions of smart, educated Christians today who all believe the Bible to be the very Word of God. You stand with some of the smartest, most influential heroes of human history, who shared our belief that the Bible is the very Word of God and therefore the standard for all we do and believe.

We Conform Our Lives to Scripture

Jesus used the Scriptures to validate His own authority. He clearly expressed that His followers are not to ignore the Scriptures but to live them out to completion.

> Do not think that I have come to abolish the Law or the Prophets;
> I have not come to abolish them but to fulfill them. For truly I tell

you, until heaven and earth disappear, not the smallest letter, not
the least stroke of a pen, will by any means disappear from the Law
until everything is accomplished. (Matthew 5:17–18)

The Bible is not merely a human book. Every prophecy in Scripture originated in God's Holy Spirit.

For prophecy never had its origin in the human will, but prophets,
though human, spoke from God as they were carried along by the
Holy Spirit. (2 Peter 1:21)

The New Testament Scriptures are just as God-breathed as the
Gospels about Jesus's life and the books of the Old Testament.

When you received the word of God, which you heard from us,
you accepted it not as a human word, but as it actually is, the
word of God, which is indeed at work in you who believe. (1 Thes-
salonians 2:13)

In the simplest sense, the same Scriptures that led you to salvation
will continue reshaping you and guiding you as you follow Christ.

If you really want to live the Christian life, the Bible is what
will keep you in God's restoration shop, so that He can continue
making you a "new creation." When you read and obey the words
of Scripture, you are choosing to remain underneath God's good,
loving, and knowing hands, so that He can continue reshaping
you in every way.

The Scriptures lead us to salvation by explaining that Jesus is God
and that He died on the cross for our sins. We know that those things
are historically verifiable. We do not believe them *only* because the
Bible tells us so. We believe them because they are facts. They are
true. And these spiritual truths work in real life—in our lives and
the lives of millions of other people. And yet, if we did not have
the Bible, we would not know what to make of these historic facts.

Then, once we come to salvation, we start to realize that the Word
of God is true. It is trustworthy. If we want God to supernaturally

change us for the better, then we look to the Scriptures—and they reshape us one day at a time as we follow Christ.

> But as for you, continue in what you have learned and have become convinced of. . . . You have known the Holy Scriptures, which are able to make you wise for salvation through faith in Christ Jesus. (2 Timothy 3:14–15)

If you've believed in Jesus while reading this book, or if this book has affirmed and confirmed your belief in Jesus, that verse above captures my desire for you: to continue with what you have learned.

Paul the Apostle described that either our thinking will be "conformed" to the popular but dead-end thinking of the culture around us, or our thinking will be "transformed." *How do we transform our thinking?* By renewing our minds in the words and promises of Scripture. It is only through the "renewing" of our minds that we are able to fully live up to God's "good, pleasing and perfect will" (Romans 12:1–2).

The Word of God Protects Us from Pain

My daughter Zoey's name comes from the ancient Greek word that means "life," and she is true to her name. Wherever Zoey goes, she brings life and energy, joy and laughter. While this is usually a good thing, Zoey has found herself in some situations where she needed to restrain and direct the life that bursts forth from her personality.

When Zoey was three years old, there was a period of a few months when she would often take off running unpredictably and uncontrollably. This could be cute in a safe, padded place. But sometimes Zoey would take off running in places that were dangerous, like parking lots. We would park the car, get Zoey out of her seat—and as soon as we set her on the pavement, she would take off running at full speed.

As fun as this may have *felt* for Zoey as a three-year-old, it was often dangerous. Her young mind was not aware of the cars and trucks driving through the parking lot.

I remember one time in particular when we had parked at a large shopping center. As our little family began getting out of the car, I looked away for what seemed like only a second. Next thing I knew, Zoey was darting out in front of a giant Chevy Suburban.

In that moment, the way I expressed love to Zoey was not to gently whisper to her. It was not to encourage her to follow her heart, nor was it to sing her a lullaby.

No, in that moment, the best expression of love was my running to her, grabbing her arm with a firm grip, and pulling her out of the way of the SUV.

When God says that He gave us Scripture to "rebuke" us (see 2 Timothy 3:16), the idea is not God coming down on us because He is mad at us. Instead, the idea is God as a loving Father saying, *Whoa, whoa, don't go there! That thing will destroy you. That sin will destroy your relationship with your kids. That person will destroy your marriage—don't go there.*

When we are reading the Word of God and opening our hearts, the Word of God corrects us like that. It trains us in right living. This protects us and allows us to function as we were designed to function.

Scripture Shows Us the Way

For any follower of Jesus who wants to stay clear of traps and wasted years of life, God's Word is the map that will guide and protect us.

> How can a young person stay on the path of purity?
> By living according to your word. I seek you with all my
>   heart;
>   do not let me stray from your commands.

I have hidden your word in my heart
    that I might not sin against you. (Psalm 119:9–11)

In part 3 of this book, when we learned about God restoring us, we learned that the restoration of a classic car often begins with its engine. As the engine and power train get refurbished, the car can once again do what it was originally designed to do.

In a similar way, as you follow Jesus and allow the Word of God to reshape you, it will rebuild you so you can function as originally designed. The Word of God trains you to actually live as you were intended to live.

As you obey it, the Word of God will change your life in every dimension: your relationships, your thoughts, your habits, and your choices. These changes affect the trajectory of your life and legacy—for the better. As God restores your thinking, you can start to race again. You can start to do what you were designed to do and experience the fulfillment and purpose God designed for you.

In a world that is shaking, shifting, dangerous, and unsettling, God wants to make you stable. Even more than that, God has good works for you to do.[3] God wants to make you fruitful. He wants to make you a light in the darkness.

God is going to use you in your environments and in your life. He will do this as you submit yourself to the Word of God and allow it to refine and improve you.

Scripture is our repair manual

I've worked to repair and restore a few different cars, and I'll admit one of my common mistakes is that I often start the project without a repair manual, thinking I can figure it all out on my own. But I often get to a point where I cannot figure something out. A point where it seems like "There is no way to remove this part" or "There is no way to reach in there."

In those moments I surrender my pride and finally look to the manual. The repair manual is great because it is written by the people who designed the car and know how to completely take it apart and put it back together.

Scripture functions like a repair manual for our lives. It tells us exactly what behaviors to take off and to put on. When we get stuck in our thought life, in our finances, or in any other area of life, Scripture gives us step-by-step instructions.[4]

Just like a repair manual, the Word of God shows us what needs to change. It also shows us a picture of what the final restored product will look like. Yes, God has given us a complete and human picture of what our full restoration will look like in the person of Jesus.

In Jesus's life we find interactions, dialogue, and stories that reveal what a fully restored human looks like—free from sin and fully connected to God. When we're not sure how to respond to a situation, we can look at how Jesus treated people, and we can look at how Jesus prayed to the Father.

Just like someone restoring a car might have a poster of that restored car on the wall of the garage, we have a picture of our restoration when we look at Jesus. We can look at Him and say, "That's what I'm going for. That's what I want to be like. With God's help, that's what I *will* be like."

Repair manuals are also helpful because sometimes we know what to do but don't know *how* to do it. That happens in the Christian life too. We often think, *Okay, I know that thing is not good for me, but I don't know how to stop doing it.* When that happens, we can look to the repair manual of God's Word. Even better, we can join a group of other believers who are also reading the manual. The best groups of believers share how they've grown in a process that helps every person in the group experience God's victory.

Like the Bible, repair manuals are thick books. Don't let this intimidate you. Instead, let it encourage you. What it means is this: your full restoration will not happen overnight. It can take years and years of working on a car to restore it.

In the case of your Christian life, you will be a work in progress until you arrive safely in heaven. When you find another area of your life that is not where you or God want it to be, don't get discouraged. When you find some new sin in your heart or uncover some ugly stuff in your life, don't get depressed. Don't get down on yourself. The repair manual assures us that none of us are fully restored overnight. Every restoration project is a work in progress, and every follower of Jesus is also a work in progress.

Scripture is a map that guides us

The Word of God is also like a map. Here's what I've noticed with maps. Whether you use a paper map, a road atlas, or a driving-directions app like Waze, MapQuest, Google Maps, or Apple Maps, you end up trusting the people who put that map or app together.

When you select a map or app, you are trusting that those mapmakers knew what they were doing. As a result, you follow their directions. You may have moments of driving when you think, *Well, my gut really tells me I should go right, but the map is saying I should go left.* But no matter how you feel, you should trust the map.

And that's how it is with the Word of God in our lives. There are times when we think, *I really want to go right, but God's Word is telling me to go left.* Here's the thing: you can trust the Word of God in those situations. A map or app may occasionally be incorrect, but the Bible never is.

In fact, because of the "ruined" or fallen and deceitful part of us, it is crucial that we choose to trust the Word of God. The growing follower of Jesus says, "I'm going to trust the Word of God more than I trust my own heart. I'm going to trust God's heart more than I trust my heart. I trust that He is bigger. He has a bigger view, and He knows me. I can actually trust God and His guidance for my life. I trust God's Word more than I trust my own feelings, which change from day to day and season to season."

We Teach the Word

Because we follow Jesus, we teach His Word to ourselves and others. At the beginning of this book we looked at Jesus's final command to His disciples, His "Great Commission," when He told us:

> All authority in heaven and on earth has been given to me. Therefore go and make disciples of all nations, baptizing them in the name of the Father and of the Son and of the Holy Spirit, and *teaching them to obey everything I have commanded you.* And surely I am with you always, to the very end of the age. (Matthew 28:18–20)

This book is a step toward learning and teaching Jesus's followers "to obey everything" He commanded. A next step for each of us is reading Jesus's words directly in the Bible. Read them regularly and obey them.

We first obey Jesus's command to be "teaching" by learning ourselves: reading Jesus's words consistently, and then doing what He says.

As we "go and make disciples," we informally teach our children, our friends, our spouses, and other believers the importance of reading and obeying Jesus's words. When we become spiritual parents to new believers or when we become physical parents to a new generation, God entrusts us with the responsibility to train the next generation in the life-or-death importance of His Word.

Jesus promised great reward for anyone who teaches others to obey His commands.

> Therefore anyone who sets aside one of the least of these commands and teaches others accordingly will be called least in the kingdom of heaven, *but whoever practices and teaches these commands will be called great in the kingdom of heaven.* (Matthew 5:19)

Jesus is looking for followers who will take His Word seriously. He is looking for those who will "teach others" to love and obey the Scriptures. This teaching does not need to be from a stage or using a microphone or screen. In fact, the best teaching of this kind takes place in coffee shops, living rooms, text messages, and one-on-one conversations about how to follow Jesus. God promises eternal reward and greatness in the kingdom of heaven for anyone who teaches growing believers how to follow His commands.

At the conclusion of the Bible, in the book of Revelation, God gives a strong warning to anyone who would mock, minimize, or take away from His Word.

> And if anyone takes words away from this scroll of prophecy, God will take away from that person any share in the tree of life and in the Holy City, which are described in this scroll. (22:19)

As followers of Jesus, we make the Word of God the standard for what we do and believe. We follow it as our guide. We trust it as our anchor. We do so because Jesus did.

> These commandments that I give you today are to be on your hearts. Impress them on your children. Talk about them when you sit at home and when you walk along the road, when you lie down and when you get up. (Deuteronomy 6:6–7)

If we meet people who claim to be Christians or Jesus followers but they do not value the Word of God as their standard, we can lovingly show them what Jesus said about the Scriptures, as we have seen in this part of the book. Whether they choose to agree with us or not, we can choose to continue following Jesus by loving and obeying His Word.

Here is a closing prayer to move this truth from your mind to your heart:

Dear Jesus,

As I follow You, I want to fully experience my new identity in You. I know that Your Word is the tool to keep me connected to Your truth and keep me experiencing Your power. Will You help me love Your Word as You do? Will You help me read it regularly? Will You help me obey it as a way of life?

Jesus, just as You did, I choose to make the Scriptures the standard for all I will do and believe. When I need to figure out what I believe about any issue or situation, I will look to Your Word to shape my beliefs.

Jesus, help me when Your path is different from the path of my friends, classmates, family, coworkers, or society. Help me be true to the heart of the Father—just as You were when You walked this earth.

Jesus, I know the Bible expresses the very heart of God. I cannot claim to love and follow You if I don't take Your words seriously. Help me love Your words and live out the life of freedom they make possible. Amen.

14

God's Love Letter to You

Do I Really Need to Believe the Bible to Live in God's Power?

Next time you're at a Super Bowl party, here's something you can look for. Did you know that when an NFL quarterback runs onto the field, they are carrying a book with them? It's true. Most pro quarterbacks carry a small playbook on their wrist in the form of a plastic-covered wristband. That tiny flap of paper is a printed summary of the team's most important plays.

Why do NFL teams do this? Because when the team goes out onto the field, they don't know exactly what is going to happen. But they do know that their strategists and coaches have already thought of a play for anything that could happen. That playbook can instruct them in any potential scenario.

The Word of God works the same way in our lives. When we head out to work, to school, or into another day, we don't know for sure what challenges we will face. But God's Word is like a playbook. There's no situation that could come our way that God has not already thought through. And God has already created a winning play for us in that situation.

In the Word of God you have a playbook full of winning scenarios, if you will follow the plays. Anything that comes your way in your finances, health, work, or relationships—God has already written a play for you to handle it.

But this playbook is not going to do you any good if you are not reading it. God encourages us to open the Bible and open our hearts to His voice within it. Reading and obeying the Bible does not earn our salvation. Rather, it continues the restoration process God began when we received the free gift of salvation. As Scriptures states, "For God is working in you, giving you the desire and the power to do what pleases him" (Philippians 2:13 NLT).

Reading and obeying the Word of God keeps us plugged into this power of God in our lives. Reading and obeying the Word of God is for our benefit; it's for our good. To continue being restored, we open up the Word of God, and we open our hearts and say, "God, reshape me today. Reshape my desires. Help me live up to my identity as a new creation, as an adopted child of God in Your family."

A Reliable Guide

Here's the great news: as a follower of Jesus in a world that is constantly changing and divided, you have an unchanging and reliable guide. God's Word has been proven faithful and reliable for thousands of years.

The Bible is not some boring rule book that constrains your life and makes it smaller. Instead, the Bible's pages direct your feet to remain on the path of freedom. The Bible directs your choices, protecting you from traps, keeping you on the road that leads to fullness of life.

One believer whom God used to write part of the Bible experienced the big life that results from obeying Scripture. God's Spirit moved him to write:

> I run in the path of your commands,
> for you have broadened my understanding. (Psalm
> 119:32)

In other words, when you follow God's "commands" in the Bible, your life opens up larger. You run in the path of freedom as He makes your life bigger.

God will guide you through the rubble and debris of the world. Sometimes following Jesus will be a narrow road, but His narrow road always leads to wide-open spaces, where you have peace and joy and healthy relationships you would not have apart from Christ.

Following God's Word doesn't mean you will never get sick or never have problems, but it does mean that internally you will always have supernatural peace. You will become a different and better person, "a new creation." As you stay on God's road for your life, He will be with you through all the ups and downs.

God's Word is a guidebook that will protect you. For your own good, He expects you to take His Word seriously and "obey" it.

> You have laid down precepts
> that are to be fully obeyed. (Psalm 119:4)

I have seen the power of God's Word in my own life. Years ago, I began the practice of treating the Bible as if it were a love letter from my Creator.

I read the Bible or listen to it on my Audible app, hearing it as loving words of guidance from my Good Father. This practice has connected the Word of God to my heart in a way that has directed me through major decisions, steadied me through times of crisis, and ultimately shaped my life for the better.

My marriage, career, children—my entire life—would not have stability and fruitfulness today if not for the Word of God and the guidance it gives me daily.

In any given week, I have dozens of matters where my old nature wants to go one way but God's Word says to go a different way, a better way. Following God's Word—instead of my heart—has always led to a better result.

I do my best when I say to God, "Okay, if You say to go left, then even if I feel like going right, I will go Your way. God, if You say, 'go back,' I'm going to turn around. I'm going to obey You."

I don't do this perfectly. No believer does. But imperfect people can still make meaningful decisions. We can decide, "I'm going to side with the Word of God. When my heart and the Bible disagree, the Bible is going to win." This choice, which I must remake daily and in each new season of life, has put me on the path of freedom that God describes.

I have seen this proven true not only in my own life but also in the lives of friends, coworkers, entire families, and larger groups of people. And I want to encourage you. If you've never made this decision before, decide today that "I'm going to do what God's Word says so that I can experience His power."

Plant Your Roots in His Word

I love taking walks by the water. I grew up in an area of Michigan defined by lakes and rivers, and I've noticed something when I walk by them. There are always giant trees right at the edge of the water.

Have you ever noticed this?

Why are there so many big trees on lakeshores and riverbanks?

All trees need sunlight, but if you go to the desert, where there is plenty of sun, you will not find big trees like this. The reason you find big trees by the water is that trees need water. Water is the power source and lifeblood of a tree.

A massive tree next to a lake is perfectly situated because it can drink and drink, constantly growing. Sometimes you can even see a large tree's roots reaching down into the water.

This is how God describes His Word in Psalm 1. God says that "blessed" is the person who delights in Scripture. Blessed is the person who, when they are not sure what to do, searches the Word of God first instead of searching Facebook or Instagram or asking a friend.

A tree that reaches its roots into a lake will grow big and strong, much stronger than a tree that's not feeding on an unlimited water source. In the same way, a believer who reaches their roots into the Word of God will grow big and strong, much stronger than a believer who is not feeding on the unlimited source of God's wisdom.

God promises in Psalm 1 that the person who delights in the law of the Lord (the Bible) will be like a tree that is planted by rivers of living water. That person will have a fruitful life. That person's leaves will be green and will not wither.[1] That person will bear fruit in season.

I have seen this in my life and also witnessed this, over the course of decades, in the lives of my grandpa and my dad. Neither were perfect men. But both lived rich lives of helping others, and the common theme was their daily reading and obeying the Word of God.

One of Jesus's greatest followers, Paul the Apostle, ended his ministry with the same message. When he wrote his final letter of spiritual guidance, at the very end of his life, Paul said (and I am paraphrasing here): "Timothy, I've taught you everything I know about serving Christ. Now here is the most important thing: 'All Scripture is from God and it is useful and profitable. It will teach you. It will correct you. It will rebuke you, it will train you in righteousness'" (see 2 Timothy 3:15–17).

In other words, Timothy, everything else you need to know is contained in the Scriptures.

Read and Obey as a Way of Life

When we choose to read and obey God's Word, it will:

Protect us from evil.

Guide us into life.

Transform us for the better.

Restore us to be who God desires us to be.

Dig your roots down deep into God's Word, and it will shape you. It will make you the best version of yourself.

When you choose to feed on God's Word, it protects you from evil. When you open your heart to God's Word, it guides you into life. It transforms you for the better.

God's Word restores your mind from the old life to the new.

Do not conform to the pattern of this world, but be transformed *by the renewing of your mind*. Then you will be able to test and approve what God's will is—his good, pleasing and perfect will. (Romans 12:2)

When you renew your mind in the Word of God, it reshapes your thinking, which reshapes your feelings, your choices, your habits, and your interactions—the very course of your life.

God's Word gives you the endurance, encouragement, and hope you need to follow Jesus in a world that is broken.

For everything that was written in the past was written to teach us, so that through the endurance taught in the Scriptures and the encouragement they provide we might have hope. (Romans 15:4)

God's Word has the power to refresh your soul. You can trust it. It is perfect and will make you wise.

The law of the LORD is perfect,
refreshing the soul.
The statutes of the LORD are trustworthy,
making wise the simple.
The precepts of the LORD are right,
giving joy to the heart.
The commands of the LORD are radiant,
giving light to the eyes.
The fear of the LORD is pure,
enduring forever.
The decrees of the LORD are firm,
and all of them are righteous.
They are more precious than gold,
than much pure gold;
they are sweeter than honey,
than honey from the honeycomb.
By them your servant is warned;
in keeping them there is great reward. (Psalm 19:7–11)

If you don't have a Bible you enjoy reading, I recommend getting *The Life Application Study Bible*. This format brought the Bible to life for me. You can search for topics in the back, and every passage of Scripture includes "application" notes beneath, just like having a really great pastor or teacher with you. It's available anywhere books are sold, including online, in a number of trustworthy Bible translations. The New International Version (NIV) and the New Living Translation (NLT) are both good choices for your first Bible.

While it's true that you can read the Bible on your phone, and there are many great Bible apps available today, I find something special in opening a physical Bible. For one thing, no distracting news or social media notifications pop onto the page while I'm trying to focus. The printed Bible also helps me focus because it doesn't have a clock staring down at me from the top of the screen, reminding me of the time.

My times with the Word of God work best when I find a private location, just as I would do to meet intimately with a best friend or confidant.

Find a time each day that works best for you. Maybe you leave your Bible right next to your bed and have time with God before you fall asleep. Or if you're a morning person, you might read it at the breakfast table. Perhaps you can leave your Bible on your work desk so you can meet with God during your lunch break. I also recommend leaving your phone or other devices in another room (or in a drawer) so you can focus 100 percent on opening your heart to God and hearing from Him.

Create a rhythm

Early in my Christian life I was intimidated by how big the Bible looks. That's when a friend told me, "Here's what I do. Start reading about Jesus's life in the Gospel of John. Every day just read until something speaks to you. Then write that one thing down, and write a prayer to God, asking Him to help you live out that one thing. The next day, pick up where you left off, and just read until something speaks to you again. And repeat."

I began doing this, and it worked. This simple practice delivered the Bible into my life in bite-size pieces I could understand and digest. I got a blank notebook and began writing the day's date and the Scripture I read. For example, "John 1:1–10." Then I would write one simple thing I'd learned about Jesus or about myself, and I would pray. This entire exercise can be done in five to fifteen minutes.

What I most enjoy about this practice of "read until something speaks to you," is that the next day, when I open up my little journal, I can look back at what God had taught me the day before. With time, I began writing out longer prayers to God in that journal, and I also began processing my decisions and my emotions with God, using His Word and prayer like a mentor or a good friend.

I began talking to God about my relationships, my hopes and dreams, and my desires. You can do the same.

You don't have to write your prayers out to be a growing Christian. For me, writing my prayers with a pen helps me focus. It centers my attention. Doing this daily has helped me experience God. It also helps my mind focus and not wander when I'm praying.

Decide where to start

When you start the habit of regular Bible reading, do not start at the beginning. I repeat, do not start in Genesis. One of the best places to start is in the Gospel of John. Other great books to begin with include Ephesians, Philippians, Colossians, Matthew, Mark, and Luke. There are sixty-six of these books in the Bible, and your Bible will list them on a contents page.

Remember, you don't have to read an entire book, or even an entire chapter, at once. Just read until something speaks to you. Then write down that one thing, pray about it, and ask God to help you live it out for the next day.

The Bible has two major sections. The second half, which is really only the final 20 percent or so, is the New Testament. That's the part most directly written to us. It is easier for us to understand and live out.

The Old Testament is also the Word of God, but just like babies cannot eat steak (because they do not have teeth), it takes some growing for us to understand, digest, and enjoy the Old Testament. You're free to read it, of course. Just know that if you can't quite chew it, this is normal, and the solution is to read some books in the New Testament a few times before carving into the steak of the Old Testament.

Make it a habit

Experts say it takes twenty-one days to create a habit. Here are a few tips to make Bible reading a positive habit.

1. Pick a consistent time (daily) when you will do your Bible reading. This could be breakfast, lunch, bedtime—it doesn't matter. The consistency is what matters. So pick a time that is realistic in your daily routine. If you know exactly when you will read your Bible every day, and you put it on your calendar or planner, you're well on your way.

2. Establish a consistent place. Just like you want to read the Bible at the same time each day, pick a place that is comfortable for you. A place that is free from distractions, realistic for your schedule, and offers the amount of privacy your personality needs. This could be a specific table or chair in your living space or your breakfast table. If you work well in coffee shops or public spaces, maybe with headphones on, that can work too.

3. Resist the trap of perfectionism or false guilt. If you miss a day, don't beat yourself up. Just get back to it.

4. Don't aim too high. Just read until you find that one thing you can apply for the day.

5. Be optimistic. God wants to meet with you daily. Ask Him to help you open your heart. Ask Him to speak to you from His Word. Make the effort for the twenty-one days it takes to build a habit. Put in the time, and you will begin hearing the Word of God speak directly to you.

Here's a formula to help you cement your plan into place:

Starting in the book of: _____,
I will read my Bible at this time: _____
and in this place: _____
until I find something that applies to me, every day.

Choose what to do during your scheduled time

Read your Bible until you read something that makes sense and hits home. Then stop there. Write the date, the chapter, and maybe the verse number. As I said before, I often write out the words of the specific verse that spoke to me, and then I write a short prayer asking God to help me live it out.

For example, let's say the verse that speaks to me is this one:

Flee the evil desires of youth and pursue righteousness, faith, love and peace, along with those who call on the Lord out of a pure heart. (2 Timothy 2:22)

Okay, I think, *that is something I can live out today.* So then I write that verse in my journal, underneath that day's date, and then I might write a prayer like this:

Second Timothy 2:22 says, "Flee the evil desires of youth and pursue righteousness, faith, love and peace, along with those who call on the Lord out of a pure heart."

God, today, will You help me flee evil desires and lusts? Please help me pursue righteousness and learn what that means. This verse says to pursue You with those who call on You from a pure heart. Help me reach out today to the people in my life who are also pursuing You. Use me to encourage them in seeking You, and use them to help me too.

Just pray that one truth from the Bible into your life. Ask for God's help, and then go out and live it, believing God gave you that truth on that day for a specific reason. The emphasis isn't how much you can read but going and living it out.

Build on your habit

In time, you'll see that God often leads you to a passage that speaks directly to a conflict, emotion, temptation, or difficulty you are facing. You will also find that, just like physical exercise, you will get stronger the more you do this. The more Scripture you read, the more it will make sense to your heart and your life.

Just as a baby goes from drinking milk to eating soft foods to eventually chewing meat, in the same way your appetite for the Word of God will grow. Having that *Life Application Study Bible* or a similar resource will help you understand what God is saying and what it means for you. You can use the tools in a study Bible to begin tracing themes, ideas, and topics in the Bible, seeing how different passages of Scripture connect with you.

The most important truths of Scripture are simple enough for a child to understand. At the same time, the Word of God is deep enough for brilliant people like Isaac Newton and Blaise Pascal to study for decades.

The Word is sort of like the ocean; you can explore all its depths if you want, or you can play in the waves at the beach. In all of it, know that God's Word is practical. It directs you. It is personal and emotional. This is a real love letter, written from your Creator to you, designed to give you the guidance, inspiration, hope, direction, and protection you need in every season of life.

God's Love Letter to You

I once heard the story of a woman who had a distant relative dying from cancer. As she visited this relative, he was kind and gentle. He was a good listener. She began to tell him all her troubles. She began to tell him things that she hadn't told anyone else, ever. She connected emotionally as she shared her fears, her regrets, her failures, and her dreams.

In the next week, as that relative was dying, he made a point to say goodbye to the woman's daughters. He said goodbye to her husband, too, and to other family members. He gave each of them heartfelt and meaningful goodbyes. Then he died.

At his funeral service, this woman stood up. She talked about how great this man was and how great a listener he was, but, she explained, she was mad at him. Mad that when he knew he was dying, he went out of his way to give a special word, a meaningful goodbye, to everyone else in the family but not to her.

"I feel left out," she said. "I feel kind of angry because he never said goodbye to me. He never spoke that word to me."

I wonder, Do you ever feel like God has forgotten you in this way? Do you ever feel like He's given other people a special word, but not you?

Do you ever feel like God hasn't thought of you?

If you have, I want to encourage you to open your eyes and open your heart to the Word of God. If you do, you will find that God is speaking directly to you every time you take the time to listen.

That woman who was so upset that her relative did not give her a meaningful goodbye—well, a few days after the funeral, she was opening her mail. And in the mail was a postcard. It was from that relative who had given everyone else a personal goodbye.

And this postcard wasn't addressed to the family. It wasn't addressed to everyone. It was addressed to her individually.

In that postcard, this relative wrote very personal, emotional, and specific words about his one-on-one relationship with her. When she read the postcard, the woman realized she had not been forgotten. This relative whom she had grown to love had thought about her and had a word just for her. She clutched that postcard to her chest, and her eyes welled up with tears.

Here's what I want you to know as a follower of Jesus: God has sent you a postcard in the Word of God. If you will clutch His Word to your chest, then you will hear your Father speaking to you individually.

Open your heart to God's Word. Be real and say, "God, here's where I am frustrated. Here's where life doesn't make sense. Will You speak to me from Your Word?"

I have learned that God always has a personal word for me in Scripture. It will be deeply emotional and specific and actually make sense in my life—but I only find these words when I take the time to open the Bible and open my heart with expectation.

If I could rewind the video of my life, I could take you to specific locations and physical places where I have met with God over and over again, in every season of my life.

These are places where I heard God speak to me from His love letter, the Bible. I could take you to a specific mountain that overlooks Scottsdale, Arizona. I would climb a trail up that mountain as the sun was setting, and I would take a little lawn chair, my Bible, and my little journal.

I could take you to riversides in Michigan. I could take you to libraries in South Carolina. I could take you to bagel shops in New York City. I could take you to benches and creeks, to La-Z-Boy reclining chairs and breakfast nooks, to specific coffee shop tables. Everywhere life has ever taken me, everywhere I have ever gone, even when I am humanly alone, my Father has always been with me. He speaks to me and guides me. All of this is possible because of the love letter He has written to me.

He has written it to you too.

God wants you to experience this daily relationship with Him. These moments are an appetizer, a preview, a glimpse of the relationship we will have with God in heaven, through Jesus.

What God tells you in the Bible is practical and helpful. It is also deeply emotional and affirming. It tells you who you are. It tells you what your purpose is. It assures you that you are loved and that you belong. It gives you stability and reminds you of your good future.

I have experienced God the most when I have most often opened His Word.

Because we love our God, we love His words to us

You can hold on to God's Word when you don't know what to do in your life. When you're paralyzed by fear of failure, God's Word can give you peace.

When you're experiencing failure or disappointment, God's Word can assure you that victory will be yours in the end, in Jesus.

When you don't know what to do as a parent, when you're trapped in sin, when you lack energy or motivation—in every emotion of life you experience, God will always be there. He's waiting to speak to you.

No matter what season you are in today, your Father wants to speak to you.

Can someone be a Christian without reading the Bible?

I am sometimes asked if reading the Bible is really necessary to be a Christian. Technically, I suppose the answer is "maybe." I mean, we're adopted into the family of God whether we read His Word or not. Our salvation does not depend on our performance as a daily Bible reader. We don't have to read the Bible to earn God's love. But . . .

Do you want to have conversations where you hear from your Creator?

Do you want to have a tight, growing relationship with your Father?

Do you want to become the best version of yourself?

Do you want to be fully restored as a new creation?

Do you want to be protected from evil?

Do you want to live more like Jesus and less like a ruin?

If so, begin to love His Word. The Word of God expresses the heart of God.

The most important thing I can say is this: don't fool yourself into thinking you really love God if you don't care about what He has to say.

Phrased more encouragingly: as you take God's words seriously, you will grow in your love relationship with your Creator. God does have specific wisdom for you. He knows the challenges you face today, and He knows the unexpected challenges you will face tomorrow. He has anticipated them. He has written to you a wise and practical love letter. He has given you a road map, a repair manual, a playbook to guide you through anything that life will throw at you.

Jesus loves me, this I know, *for the Bible tells me so.*

Here is a closing prayer to move this truth from your mind to your heart:

Father,

I thank You that the Bible is a love letter. Thank You for expressing Your love to me and speaking to me individually when I open my heart to Your Word.

Lord, help me be a believer who is committed to Your Word because I'm committed to You. Please make me a person who loves Your Word.

I believe You are God. I know You died on the cross for me. I've placed my faith in You. I know You are restoring me every day. Now, Lord, I surrender to staying in Your repair shop. I invite Your Word to do its work in me.

God, I surrender to Your Word and I ask, Will You help me to get into the habit of feeding on Your Word daily, so I can be fully restored and renewed and reshaped from the inside out?

Plant in my heart a love for Your Word. Help me study it and obey it in every season of life.

I pray this in the power and name of Jesus. Amen.

15

Key Scriptures on "For the Bible Tells Me So"

We choose the Bible as the unchanging standard for all we do and believe because Jesus did. We must read and obey the Word of God to realize our identity in Christ.

Jesus said that the Scriptures come directly from the mouth of God.

> Jesus answered, "It is written: 'Man shall not live on bread alone, but on every word that comes from the mouth of God.'" (Matthew 4:4)

Jesus modeled that the Scriptures provide power to avoid deadly temptation. He claimed that humans can and should feed on the Word of God as eagerly as we feed on physical food.

> Jesus answered, "It is written: 'Man shall not live on bread alone, but on every word that comes from the mouth of God.'" (Matthew 4:4)

Jesus claimed that every word of Scripture is fixed in the universe—more so than the very planet we walk upon.

It is easier for heaven and earth to disappear than for the least stroke of a pen to drop out of the Law. (Luke 16:17)

Jesus used the Scriptures to validate His own authority. In the same statement, He said that His life and followers are not about ignoring the Scriptures but about living them out to completion.

Do not think that I have come to abolish the Law or the Prophets; I have not come to abolish them but to fulfill them. For truly I tell you, until heaven and earth disappear, not the smallest letter, not the least stroke of a pen, will by any means disappear from the Law until everything is accomplished. (Matthew 5:17–18)

Jesus said that He is looking for followers who will take the Word of God seriously and will "teach others" to also love and obey it. Jesus promised eternal reward for His followers who love God's Word and teach others to do the same.

Therefore anyone who sets aside one of the least of these commands and teaches others accordingly will be called least in the kingdom of heaven, but whoever practices and teaches these commands will be called great in the kingdom of heaven. (Matthew 5:19)

All of the Bible has been breathed by God, for our benefit, to equip us in serving Him.

All Scripture is God-breathed and is useful for teaching, rebuking, correcting and training in righteousness, so that the servant of God may be thoroughly equipped for every good work. (2 Timothy 3:16–17)

The Word of God provides us with endurance, encouragement, and hope as we follow Jesus in a world that is broken.

For everything that was written in the past was written to teach us, so that through the endurance taught in the Scriptures and the encouragement they provide we might have hope. (Romans 15:4)

Every prophecy in Scripture originated in God's Holy Spirit.

> For prophecy never had its origin in the human will, but prophets, though human, spoke from God as they were carried along by the Holy Spirit. (2 Peter 1:21)

The New Testament Scriptures are just as God-breathed as the Gospels about Jesus's life and the Old Testament prophets.

> When you received the word of God, which you heard from us, you accepted it not as a human word, but as it actually is, the word of God, which is indeed at work in you who believe. (1 Thessalonians 2:13)

God's Word is a guidebook that will protect us. Jesus expects His followers to take it seriously and obey it.

> You have laid down precepts
> that are to be fully obeyed. (Psalm 119:4)

When we follow God's commands in the Bible, our lives open up. We run in the path of freedom as He makes our lives bigger.

> I run in the path of your commands,
> for you have broadened my understanding. (Psalm 119:32)

The words of God in the Bible are without error in all they teach us.

> And the words of the LORD are flawless,
> like silver purified in a crucible,
> like gold refined seven times. (Psalm 12:6)

For any follower of Jesus who wants to stay clear of traps and wasted years of life, God's Word is the map that will guide and protect us.

> How can a young person stay on the path of purity?
> By living according to your word.

I seek you with all my heart;
　　do not let me stray from your commands.
I have hidden your word in my heart
　　that I might not sin against you. (Psalm 119:9–11)

As followers of Jesus, we feed on God's Word, using it as our guide. We also teach others to do so.

These commandments that I give you today are to be on your hearts. Impress them on your children. Talk about them when you sit at home and when you walk along the road, when you lie down and when you get up. (Deuteronomy 6:6–7)

God's Word has the power to refresh our souls. We can trust it. It is perfect and will make us wise.

The law of the LORD is perfect,
　　refreshing the soul.
The statutes of the LORD are trustworthy,
　　making wise the simple.
The precepts of the LORD are right,
　　giving joy to the heart.
The commands of the LORD are radiant,
　　giving light to the eyes.
The fear of the LORD is pure,
　　enduring forever.
The decrees of the LORD are firm,
　　and all of them are righteous.
They are more precious than gold,
　　than much pure gold;
they are sweeter than honey,
　　than honey from the honeycomb.
By them your servant is warned;
　　in keeping them there is great reward. (Psalm 19:7–11)

PART 6

THE POWER AND PEACE JESUS PROMISED

What Is the Role of the Holy Spirit in the Life of the Believer? Does It Really Matter If I Get the Christian Beliefs Right?

> SECTION SUMMARY: **Jesus promised that God's Holy Spirit would live in His followers, encouraging us and empowering us toward supernatural action. To experience God's power, we must live in step with His Spirit and be aligned with His gospel.**

Jesus promised His followers that the Spirit of God would help us live for Him.

And I will ask the Father, and he will give you another advocate to help you and be with you forever, *the Spirit of truth*. The world cannot accept him, because it neither sees him nor knows him. But you know him, for *he lives with you and will be in you*. (John 14:16–17)

Jesus said that the Holy Spirit, living within us, will teach us how to follow Jesus in our time. The Spirit can also aid our minds and hearts in remembering God's Word.

But the Advocate, the Holy Spirit, whom the Father will send in my name, *will teach you all things and will remind you of everything I have said to you.* Peace I leave with you; my peace I give you. I do not give to you as the world gives. Do not let your hearts be troubled and do not be afraid. (John 14:26–27)

Jesus promised that His followers would receive the Holy Spirit. The Holy Spirit is the connection to God's power in our lives.

But you will receive *power* when the Holy Spirit comes on you; and [then] you will be my witnesses in Jerusalem, and in all Judea and Samaria, and to the ends of the earth. (Acts 1:8)

Jesus modeled the necessity of the Holy Spirit's power for us to do the work of God.

God anointed Jesus of Nazareth with the Holy Spirit and *power*, and . . . he went around doing good and healing all who were under the power of the devil, because God was with him. (Acts 10:38)

The power of God works through individuals and movements that believe and obey the gospel as Jesus taught it.

For I am not ashamed of the gospel, because it is the power of God that brings salvation to everyone who believes. (Romans 1:16)

Following Jesus is more than a feeling. We follow Jesus by intentionally shaping our lives to fit everything He commanded.

Go and make disciples of all nations, baptizing them in the name of the Father, the Son and the Holy Spirit, *teaching them to obey everything I have commanded you.* (Matthew 28:18–20)

16

The Holy Spirit

What Is the Role of the Holy Spirit in the Life of the Believer?

Where I grew up, the winter season was long. So when spring and summer arrived, we were eager to venture out into the woods to play. Our favorite place was a little cabin in the woods in Canada. Canada is a land full of big water. "Real water," as I tell my Arizona friends.

I will never forget the first time I saw the raw power of moving water. My three older brothers and I had hiked through the woods to a place where a small river—maybe twenty feet wide—emptied into a large lake. The river stepped down about three waterfalls—each one ten or fifteen feet high—as it dropped down into the lake.

As kids, we called this place "the falls." It was a great place to picnic, with fantastic fishing at the bottom of the falls. All sorts of bass gathered there to feed on the critters the river washed down into the lake, and I remember just dropping in a fishing line with a live worm and pulling up bass and other fish for dinner. It was usually that easy at the falls.

At the very top of the falls, the river looked—on the surface— calm as glass. And at the water-worn rock lip, where the current rushed over the edge, the surging wake was only about fourteen inches deep.

Because we were such adventurous boys, it is not surprising that one day one of my older brothers decided to walk across this very edge of the river—right where it dropped off and became a waterfall. We had crossed the river many times on foot, but always farther back, about twenty feet from the edge. Back there the water was shallower, more spread out, and less powerful.

None of us had ventured across this very point of departure in the waterfall's drop. I remember watching my brother begin to inch his way across. I was maybe eight years old at the time and was hunting for frogs along the riverbanks above the falls.

I looked over and saw the fluorescent pink of my brother's early-1990s athletic gear. He was strong. I secretly marveled that he could inch his way across the lip of the falls like that. I knew I never could.

I glanced away, toward a frog I was chasing. Then, my ears picking up on some swift noise, I looked back at the edge of the falls. My brother was gone.

In a fraction of an instant, the power of the surging water had swept him entirely off his feet and down the ten- or fifteen-foot drop of the first falls. I yelled for my other brothers, and we all ran to the bottom.

There's a deep pool at the bottom of that first drop.

Would he be swept through that pool and down the rest of the falls?

Would he hit his head on a rock along the way?

Would he be able to pop up out of the current?

The water surged, driven down by gravity, into the deep pool where my brother had disappeared. That pool was about fifteen feet wide, its contents constantly pushed deeper into the rocks by the weight of the perpetually tumbling water.

We held our breath, waiting to see if our brother would surface.

I will confess that—as the youngest brother in a home where only the oldest boys had their own bedrooms—I may have been secretly plotting about the posters I would hang in my brother's bedroom should he not surface. I would not have minded taking over his room.

But, as fate would have it, I did not get his bedroom.[1] He popped up in that whipping pool at the bottom of the waterfall, gasping for breath like a deep-water diver, and scrambled up the edge of the slippery rocks.

My brothers and me, we're boys. We've done plenty of stupid things in our lives. But never again have we underestimated the power of moving water. Not after experiencing that life lesson.

God promises Christians a similar sweep-you-off-your-feet power, which can carry us along spiritually with a force far greater than our own strength. It is an overlooked and ignored power in the lives of most believers.

It is a power that waits to pick us up and carry us—not into terror or death but into the powerful ways of God and life. When we find ourselves unable to do what's right, or unable to say no to what's wrong, when we find ourselves unable to just hang in there and keep believing, this power is available to sweep us off our feet and carry us along in God's good ways.

I know that may sound whimsical and too good to be true, but I would not tell you about this power had I not experienced it myself.

And yes, I have experienced this soul-carrying, life-propelling power. Not only have I experienced it, but I can tell you with confidence that I would not be here, would not be writing this book or any book, would not be a civilized dad or husband or man, if it were not for the role of this power in my life.

It is a power God calls His Holy Spirit.

As you venture out to live for Jesus, there will be days when you feel like you don't have enough strength in yourself. And that is true.

I feel that way nearly every day. Sometimes it's because of physical limitations, like sickness and debilitating headaches. Other days, my will seems too weak to say no to sinful things. Still other days, I feel too weak to genuinely love the people God calls me to serve.

I have days when I lack faithfulness.

I lack resolve.

I lack faith, period.

But here is the fantastic thing I've experienced with the Holy Spirit: when I can't, the Holy Spirit can.

When I Can't, God's Spirit Can

When I can't be faithful, God's Spirit can put faithfulness in me.

When I can't _____ (fill in any good thing here), God's Spirit can _____ (that same good thing) in me.

When I can't do what's right *for* me, God's Spirit can do what's right *in* me.

The things we've learned about believing in Jesus, about reading His Word, about surrendering to His continuing "restoration" work, even about reading His Word regularly—all these truths require a spiritual energy to be put into practice. If you're like me, you will find that you do not always have the spiritual energy or focus to live out the Christian life. None of us do.

We do not have, in our fallen nature, the strength to build a life upon the truths we have learned in our journey. But here's what I have found: when I am weak; when I acknowledge that I *cannot* be faithful or live like Christ; when I humbly, honestly tell God that I *cannot* be the husband, the dad, the pastor, the writer, or even just the child of His that I want to be; *when I acknowledge to God that I* can't, *that's when His Spirit* can.

Here's the good news. You don't have enough strength in *yourself*. But with God's Spirit living in you, you actually do have enough strength. Learning to "live in the Spirit" is simply learning to unleash the Spirit of God that already lives within you as a follower of Christ.

This idea of God's Spirit carrying us along when we lack strength is not just a cute, feel-good idea. In my life, the Holy Spirit has become the difference between dead-end discouragement and dig-deep encouragement.

When you feel like you can't be faithful, when you feel like you can't trust God anymore, when you feel like you just can't, then you are way, way, way ahead of the class.

Bring your "I can't" to God and invite His Spirit to do *in you* what you cannot do *for you*. He will. I've seen it. I've experienced it.

The Moment

Do you remember the moment when you learned to whistle? I do. I remember it because I had tried to whistle for so long, but without success. I remember being so frustrated that I couldn't whistle.

Not much into whistling? How about the moment you learned to ride a bike? Or swim? Was there frustration leading up to the moment when you learned those skills?

Now, of course I could have lived a happy life without ever learning to whistle or ride a bike or swim—but I would certainly have found it a life that was also missing out. In a similar way, I believe the majority of Christians are not whistlers when it comes to the skill of "walking in the Spirit."

Many Christians have not yet had the moment when they really learn to access the Holy Spirit's power for their daily lives. Many have not yet discovered that every time they hit a dead end of frustration, the Holy Spirit is waiting to empower them to do what is right.

Just like a person can live without whistling, a Christian can trust in Jesus, be heaven-bound, and experience God's sovereign provision, and yet never learn to be led and empowered by the Spirit.

This is one of the reasons why many Christians live stuck at dead ends of frustration.

In their marriages, in their desires, in their struggles to do right or to *not* do wrong, many believers are overlooking an internal power source, the Spirit of God. It is possible to receive the gift of salvation and not yet realize the power given *at* salvation, the strength of the Holy Spirit.

Scripture describes believers—who were normal people—doing supernatural things. People just like you and me experienced God's power working in them and through them, and the theme of these true stories is the Holy Spirit being unleashed within them.

I wonder, Where in your life do you have a dead end of frustration right now? Where do you know what you should do—but you struggle to actually do it? Where have you been trying to serve God, but you're all out of strength to continue on?

Grab hold of your very real struggle. Keep it in mind as we look at some believers who had "the moment" with the Holy Spirit. These are believers who realized they could never live out God's plan for their lives. But then, the Holy Spirit did *in* them what they could not do *for* themselves.

Let's watch "The Moment," when people who couldn't, got empowered by the Spirit who could.

Example #1: The first 120 ordinary Christians

The dried black and brown blood from Jesus's beatings still covered the stone pavement in Jerusalem, where He had been whipped in the public square. Then His weary body hung on a public torture device. After this gruesome death, Jesus's followers scattered. They scurried into hidden rooms and hideaways.

Can you imagine following a spiritual leader and then seeing that leader publicly tortured and murdered?

Talk about Post-Traumatic Stress Disorder, or PTSD. These few timid Christians lived daily knowing that the same people who killed their leader also wanted to torture and kill them, the followers of Jesus.

This is where we find the first 120 Christians, in the weeks after Jesus's death and resurrection. These Christians were not looking to change the world. They were just looking to survive. They were hiding, hoping not to be dragged into the public square themselves.

Keep in mind that these first Christians were just as human as you and me. They felt all the same insecurities and emotions of defeat and insecurity as we do.

In this moment of discouragement, when these believers were feeling powerless to hold on to their faith, powerless to "go and make disciples" as Jesus had commanded them, God provided a gift of supernatural power. But not before reminding them that they could not do God's work with merely human strength.

After His resurrection, Jesus appeared to this discouraged, frightened group and gave them the outrageous command to go and change the world. He told them they would launch a viral movement in the city where they lived, Jerusalem. Jesus said that their movement would then spread from there, to the entire state, then to the whole region, and then "to the ends of the earth" (see Acts 1:8).

Here's the thing about Jesus's words to these frightened believers. He predicted that they would *not* be able to go and change the world until they had their moment with the Holy Spirit. Jesus said:

> But you will receive **power** *when the Holy Spirit comes on you*; and [then] you will be my witnesses in Jerusalem, and in all Judea and Samaria, and to the ends of the earth. (Acts 1:8)

The believers will receive *power* to change the world when? When the Holy Spirit comes upon them. They would only perform supernatural work *after* the Holy Spirit had come upon them.

If you want to study this further, you can follow Acts 1:8 to Acts 2:4 to Acts 9:31. In those three verses, Jesus promises the Holy Spirit. Then He gives the Holy Spirit. And by Acts 9:31, the church has grown to tens of thousands of people, distributed throughout the exact areas that Jesus predicted back in Acts 1:8.

What happened between Acts 1 and Acts 9? The Holy Spirit is what happened.

It's important for us to notice something. It was not just apostles or prophets who got empowered by God's Spirit to do things they could never do on their own. It was 120 *ordinary* Christians. Regular folks like you and me.

When 120 Christians couldn't change the world, God's Spirit could.

Today, God's Holy Spirit lives in every follower of Jesus. He is available to empower us in building His church and living for Jesus today. Most of these believers were not raising the dead or performing dramatic healings. They were performing the miracle of telling others about Christ and staying faithful to Christ in a time of persecution.

Example #2: Little David, the giant slayer

You've likely heard of David and Goliath. Did you know that David, who became a warrior king, was a sensitive singer-songwriter before he fought Goliath? That's right. He was a poet and a musician. Read some of his psalms, and you can see just how in touch David was with his emotions.

For such a boy to singlehandedly defeat the world's greatest hand-to-hand combatant, well, that's an incredible story. Here is my favorite line in the battle between David and Goliath:

As the Philistine moved closer to attack him, *David ran quickly toward the battle line to meet him . . .* [and] David triumphed over the Philistine. (1 Samuel 17:48, 50)

I remember playing dodgeball in gym class as a kid. The two teams lined up on opposite ends of the gymnasium. The dodgeballs were set in the middle of the gym, and when the teacher blew the whistle, the boldest, fastest kids *sprinted* to the middle. These assertive, aggressive types often grabbed one or more of the dodgeballs, preparing to wallop the rest of us.

And us average people? The rest of us, the slow, the timid, the hoping-to-survive, we never ran too fast toward that middle battle line.

In our story, we have little David the sheepherder. David the youngest. David the songwriter, who had no armor and no sword. All he had was a piece of fabric and a few rocks. And moving to the middle-field battle line was an armored, blood-stained professional killer nearly twice his height. Goliath had killed hundreds if not thousands of full-grown men in duels just like this. Goliath's sword alone was probably as long as David's legs.

And what did David do?

He *ran*. He *sprinted* toward this impossible opponent.

Now, let's pause the story here. Because something important has happened to David just *before* he ran at this impossible enemy. David just had "the moment" with the Spirit of God.

Just before David fought Goliath, we're told this:

> So Samuel [a prophet of God] took the horn of oil and anointed [David] in the presence of his brothers, and from that day on the Spirit of the LORD came upon David in *power*. (1 Samuel 16:13)

It was the Holy Spirit who empowered David in his fight against Goliath. I emphasized "power" in that sentence of Scripture, because Jesus used the same word, "power," to describe the Holy Spirit's work for the 120 Christians in Acts 1:8.

David did a lot of powerful things in his life on earth, a lot of impossible things. And Scripture is clear about the reason why. When David couldn't, God's Spirit *could*.

Example #3: Jesus Himself

If you've been going to church for a long time, you might struggle to believe example 3. But it comes straight from the pages of Scripture. *Did you know that Scripture does not record Jesus doing a single miracle in His life on earth until the Holy Spirit came upon Him?*

I'm not saying that Jesus couldn't have done a miracle without the Holy Spirit. What I am saying is that God chose, in His wisdom, to have Jesus's miracles occur *after* the Holy Spirit descended upon Him. Perhaps God did this because Jesus is our example of how we can live for God.

Our human minds struggle to understand how God could humble Himself, take the limited form of a human, and drop down among us. Scripture explains that when God lowered Himself down in the person of Jesus, He willingly reduced Himself.[2]

As a result, Jesus, being the perfect model for us, relied on the Holy Spirit's power to follow God the Father and do extraordinary things.

"The moment" is so important in Jesus's life that all four Gospels begin the story of Jesus's public ministry with the moment when the Holy Spirit publicly came into Jesus's life. Here's how the Gospel of Mark puts it:

> Just as Jesus was coming up out of the water, he saw heaven being torn open and *the Spirit descending on him like a dove.* (Mark 1:10)

All four Gospel accounts begin Jesus's earthly ministry with this scene of the Holy Spirit descending on Him.[3]

These duplicate Gospel accounts are no accident. God is showing us what a spiritually empowered human looks like. And there's no such thing as a supernaturally, spiritually powerful person of God apart from the Holy Spirit.

So, in a practical sense, even Jesus did not live like Jesus, without the Holy Spirit. That is, all the miracles we know from the

Gospels, from Jesus's public ministry, occurred after the Holy Spirit descended on Jesus.

If you disagree with that statement, you'll have to take it up with Matthew, Mark, Luke, and John. Also, you'll need to take it up with God, who tells us yet again in Scripture:

> God anointed Jesus of Nazareth with the Holy Spirit and *power*, and . . . he went around doing good and healing all who were under the power of the devil, because God was with him. (Acts 10:38)

We have now seen the word "power" in all three of these stories about God's Holy Spirit. Where the Spirit of God is, there is power. All throughout Scripture, throughout history, and throughout my own personal life, I've seen it.

These are just three examples of "the moment." Scripture holds dozens more. The point is that you can have this moment too. The moment when you begin looking to the Holy Spirit to do in you what you cannot do for yourself.

In my life, the moment did not involve anything dramatic on the outside, no wild noises or physical activity, but it was a time when I surrendered to the Spirit of God who had been living within me from the instant I believed in Jesus as my Savior.

Your moment with the Holy Spirit doesn't have to be dramatic. And it doesn't mean you will never struggle with sin or doubt again. In fact, Jesus had more emotional and physical pain *after* the Spirit came upon Him than before.[4]

But, like learning to whistle or swim, this is a moment, a turning point, when you begin acquiring a skill. It's the skill of walking in step with God's Spirit. The skill of looking immediately to the Spirit of God for power, comfort, or direction, any time you find yourself at a dead end.

When 120 ordinary Christians couldn't change the world, God's Spirit could.

When a shepherd boy couldn't defeat a trained killer, God's Spirit could.

When Jesus came to model right living on earth, even He relied on that third Person in the Trinity, the Holy Spirit.[5]

If Jesus Himself did not live like Jesus apart from the Holy Spirit, then could it be that we sometimes get frustrated in our efforts to follow Jesus because we're trying to do so without the Holy Spirit?

Left to ourselves, believers have a tendency to fall into one of two extremes when thinking of the Holy Spirit.

Some Christians think the Spirit exists primarily so we can do dramatic magic tricks. Other believers view the Holy Spirit as a set of facts on a page. They get some information about the Spirit correct, but then the Spirit makes little or no actual difference in their daily lives.

God did not give us the Holy Spirit so we could do hokey magic tricks. He also did not give us the Holy Spirit so we could merely memorize facts about Him. The Holy Spirit is the personal presence of God, available to encourage and also empower us in following Jesus.

Seize Your "Moment" with God's Spirit

God gave us the Spirit so we could follow Christ in supernatural ways. He gave us the Holy Spirit to empower us and even carry us on our journey to heaven.

Whenever God calls you to do some difficult thing, the Holy Spirit is eagerly waiting to strengthen you, so that you can do what God has called you to do.

Is God calling you to endure and be faithful?

Is God calling you to redefine the way you see yourself as His child?

Is God calling you to be bold about what you believe?

Is God calling you to surrender an area of "ruin" or brokenness in your life so that He can restore it?

Whatever God calls you to do, He will empower you toward that right action by His Holy Spirit. The choice you must make, just like the choice of learning to whistle or swim, is if you will seek "the moment" and embrace this new way of Spirit-powered living.

This moment will happen when you look to the Spirit in your dead ends of frustration. Like other learned skills, we learn, one dead end at a time, to invite the Spirit to strengthen us where we are unable.

Where are you powerless?

Powerless to be faithful?

Powerless to do some right thing?

Or powerless to not do some wrong thing?

Whatever your dead end of frustration, call out to God now. Ask specifically for His Spirit to be unleashed in that area of your life. Ask the Holy Spirit to empower you in God's paths for your life.

Just like He empowered those first 120 Christians.

Just like He empowered David.

Just like He empowered Jesus.

The Holy Spirit is alive and moving today. He is a rushing current. A raging rapid. An irresistible force. He is carrying nations and eras into God's eternal purposes. You've heard the rush of the waterfall. You've read the stories.

Time to step into the current.

Here is a prayer to help you express your desire to fully experience God's Holy Spirit in your life.

Almighty God,

You see the areas of my life where I lack the power to do Your work. You see the areas of my life where I lack peace. You see the areas of my life where I lack the comfort that Jesus promised from "the Comforter," the Holy Spirit.

Today I want to experience the power, peace, and presence of Your Spirit. I ask that You open my eyes and open my heart. I desire to live a Spirit-filled and Spirit-led life, as You describe in Your Word. I desire to see Your Spirit work powerfully in me and through me, just as You promised in Acts 1. I desire to experience the comfort and guidance of Your Spirit, as Jesus promised in John 16. Lord, I am Your servant and Your child. Thank You for giving me a power source, a source of peace and purpose in Your Spirit. Please forgive me if I have stifled or grieved Your Spirit in any way, and please teach me to walk in the fullness, freedom, and joy that You desire for me through the gift of You living in me, in the person of Your Holy Spirit. Amen.

17

The Power to Solve
Your Greatest Problems

Does It Really Matter If I Get
the Christian Beliefs Right?

The word "gospel" found in Romans 1:16 encapsulates the Christian essentials we have learned in this book.

> For I am not ashamed of the gospel, because it is the power of God that brings salvation to everyone who believes. (Romans 1:16)

In our journey we have learned precisely what a person must believe in order to experience "the power of God that brings salvation." This power of God is freely available "to everyone who believes."

God has entrusted to you this power to change the world. As a believer in Christ, you stand shoulder to shoulder with believers like the Reverend Martin Luther King Jr., Harriet Tubman, Paul the apostle, and hundreds of history's other greatest leaders who believed these same Christian essentials.

Don't let anyone make you think that being a Christian is weak or irrelevant. It wasn't weak or irrelevant for Dr. King, it wasn't weak or irrelevant for the Christians who fought to end slavery in the United States, and it sure wasn't weak or irrelevant for those early Christians in the book of Acts. Their obedience changed the course of world history.

In Christ, we have the very power of God that brings salvation.

Christians from different backgrounds, traditions, or cultures may disagree about matters of worship, personal life, or politics, but these basic essentials unite all true followers of Christ. We cling to these essential Christian beliefs, knowing that if we lose them, we lose the power of God that brings salvation.

Like the European power plug I described earlier in this book, these Christian essentials are the prongs that plug us into the power grid of the universe, almighty God.

Before I was a pastor I worked as a full-time journalist. Like many of my colleagues in the news industry, I investigated stories that had a common theme: the world's great problems. Whether the problem was drug addiction, crime, injustice, or violence, my job was to document humanity's problems and solutions.

During my early years as a journalist I began to seriously investigate Jesus. I began seeing that sincere followers of Jesus—transformed by His gospel—were often at the forefront of humanity's great needs, where I would see them serving and helping others.

I began attending Scottsdale Bible Church in Arizona. Once a month I would pile into an SUV with other young professionals from the church, and we would drive from Arizona down to Mexico. Within a number of hours, we would journey from one of the wealthiest cities in Arizona to one of the poorest slums in Mexico. There, in a village built atop an old garbage dump, I saw Christians from various churches working together to build homes for the poor.

The more I studied Jesus, His message, and His followers, the more I became convinced that Jesus's message is not only the power for individual salvation but also the greatest power for human good. I saw firsthand that Christians were starting orphanages, feeding the hungry, and working for the justice of the oppressed. I met Christians making laws in state capitals and feeding the hungry in urban ghettos.

As I grew more passionate about this, some of my non-Christian news colleagues would tease me. My zeal was making me look like a religious nutcase. These were highly educated intellectuals, and my uninhibited passion for Jesus sounded foolish to them.

It didn't matter though. I was experiencing Jesus's ability to transform me. In my church small group, I was seeing Jesus transform real people. I imagined what a society could look like if all its people experienced this heart transformation from Jesus. Such a society would not need locks or courts or prisons. It would be the kingdom Jesus described and promised in the Gospels.

God was growing my love for this gospel of Jesus. It is indeed the greatest news for humanity, and we should carry it with urgency. We have the solution to the problems everyone else is trying to solve.

One time, at a national journalism awards presentation, a national TV news anchor asked me why I would leave a promising career in journalism to become a pastor. As I answered, God brought Romans 1:16 to my mind:

> I am not ashamed of the gospel, because it is the power of God that brings salvation to everyone who believes.

That word, "gospel," literally means "the good news." I was leaving this world's news business so that I could give my life to proclaim the greatest good news ever known to humanity.

Ten years later I am still not ashamed of this good news I am experiencing. *Why not?* Because this message about Jesus is not just another belief system. It is not just one religion in a buffet of world religions. No, it is actually the power of God, and I've experienced it.

Christianity according to Christ is the power of God *that brings salvation*. That is, it brings deliverance from our own broken habits and addictions. It restores our relationship to God and creates a pathway for restored relationships with others. It brings eternal life.

Christianity according to Christ sets us free from the fear of death. One of my favorite Scriptures declares:

> Since the children have flesh and blood, [Jesus] too shared in their humanity so that by his death he might break the power of him who holds the power of death—that is, the devil—and free those who all their lives were held in slavery by their fear of death. (Hebrews 2:14–15)

Because of the truths discussed in this book, we no longer live under the fear of death. We know that eternal life is ours through Christ's work on the cross.

Christ's message is the power to change our world and ourselves for the better.

You are now equipped to confidently know and carry this message with you everywhere you go. God's nature and His Word are as vast as the galaxies He created, but the foundational truths of Christianity are not complicated.

As you carry the essential truths of Christianity with you, I want to encourage you that God has called you to be a world changer. He has a job for you in bringing about His kingdom. He has "good works," which He prepared in advance for you to do (see Ephesians 2:10).

Your "good works" today could be giving someone a cup of water in Jesus's name or representing Christ in a courtroom or classroom. Your faithful obedience to the precise good works God has set out for you will bring about the kingdom of Christ.

————————

Earlier I mentioned Martin Luther King Jr., who is one of my personal heroes. Dr. King is undoubtedly one of the greatest humanitarians and champions of civil rights in all of history. In his lifetime, he was called "Reverend" Martin Luther King Jr.

Read Dr. King's writings. Listen to his recorded sermons, and you will find that the teachings of Jesus run through them like steel beams, undergirding the way Dr. King viewed himself, the world, and society at large.

He held to the Christian essentials we have learned in this book. And it was this view of God and humanity that empowered him to be so fearless in his fight for human equality and human rights as God defines them.

The world is a better place because of the work of Jesus's words and teachings in and through Martin Luther King Jr. And he is not a rarity among sincere followers of Jesus. Millions of Jesus's followers have improved humanity in widespread ways that still benefit us today—people like Harriet Tubman, Abraham Lincoln, Frederick Douglass, and so many others who were shaped and motivated by the essential Christian beliefs.[1]

The beliefs we have learned in this book have led sincere Christians to create schools, orphanages, hospitals, social welfare systems, and human rights laws that did not exist before Christianity.

Christianity is not just a theory. Yes, it leads to eternal life, but it also makes a real difference in our present lives and world.

Because we want the people we love to have freedom, we should pass these Christian essentials from generation to generation.

I want you to imagine a community where thousands of us are plugged into this power source of the universe. As the world gets darker and darker around us—darker in hatred, greed, and immorality—as people around us wrestle with addictions and sexual abuse and hundreds of other problems, we get to bring light and warmth to them. We get to bring powerful hope. We get to travel through this broken world, not as walking theological dictionaries but as glowing lights in the darkness. Glowing because we are plugged into the Power Source.

We are able to love our neighbors. We are able to live free from selfishness and self-defeating vices. We are able to live free from death. We are able to model a life of power and purpose. We can display for our neighbors, our friends, our children, and our grandchildren that in Christ we have found "the power of God unto salvation" (Romans 1:16).

Father,

We are so thankful You injected Your power into this broken world as the Messiah. We believe You that we are now "the body" of the Messiah, placed here for a purpose: to continue bringing souls into Your kingdom.

Lord, give us a sense of purpose and courage as we carry Your gospel in this broken world. Help us to live lives that bring Your kingdom here on earth.

Keep us plugged into Your power to change our lives and change our world. Please show Your power to the people we love in our families, neighborhoods, and places of work or school. Please change the world through us, for Your glory.

Father, without Your power, we have no good thing. As the psalmist wrote in Psalm 19:14, may the words of our mouths, the meditations of our hearts, and the works of our hands be pleasing in Your sight. Empower us to accomplish Your purposes.

We have tasted and seen the power of the universe surging through us to change our thoughts, our relationships, and our lives. Please keep us plugged into Your power. Make us a people who are a bright light in this dark world.

We ask in Jesus's name, Amen.

18

Key Scriptures on "The Power and Peace Jesus Promised"

Jesus promised that God's Holy Spirit would live in His followers, encouraging us and empowering us in supernatural action. To experience God's power we must live in step with His Spirit and be aligned with His Gospel.

Jesus promised His followers that the Spirit of God would help us live for Him.

> And I will ask the Father, and he will give you another *advocate to help you and be with you forever—the Spirit of truth.* The world cannot accept him, because it neither sees him nor knows him. But you know him, for *he lives with you and will be in you.* (John 14:16–17)

Jesus said that the Holy Spirit, living within us, will teach us how to follow Jesus in our time. The Spirit can also aid our minds and hearts in remembering God's Word.

But the Advocate, the Holy Spirit, whom the Father will send in my name, *will teach you all things and will remind you of everything I have said to you.* Peace I leave with you; my peace I give you. I do not give to you as the world gives. Do not let your hearts be troubled and do not be afraid. (John 14:26–27)

Jesus said that the Holy Spirit can be so powerful in our lives that it is actually better to have the Holy Spirit living within us than to have Jesus walking alongside us.

But very truly I tell you, *it is for your good that I am going away. Unless I go away, the Advocate will not come to you; but if I go, I will send him to you.* . . . *But when he, the Spirit of truth, comes, he will guide you into all the truth.* He will not speak on his own; he will speak only what he hears, and he will tell you what is yet to come. (John 16:7, 13)

Note: According to Jesus's own words, the Holy Spirit will never lead a believer or church to do anything that contradicts Jesus's words or the words of Scripture. Instead, true movements of the Spirit will empower Jesus's people to live out His words and the words of Scripture.

Just like Jesus, we should also be led by the Holy Spirit in our daily lives.

For those who are led by the Spirit of God are the children of God. (Romans 8:14)

Since we live by the Spirit, let us keep in step with the Spirit. (Galatians 5:25)

Jesus promised that His followers would receive the Holy Spirit. The Holy Spirit is the connection to God's power in our lives.

But you will receive *power when the Holy Spirit comes on you.* (Acts 1:8)

The Holy Spirit helps us in our weakness.

The Spirit helps us in our weakness. (Romans 8:26)

When a group of believers needs spiritual encouragement from God Himself, the Holy Spirit can provide it.

Then the church throughout Judea, Galilee and Samaria enjoyed a time of peace and was strengthened. Living in the fear of the Lord and *encouraged by the Holy Spirit*, it increased in numbers. (Acts 9:31)

The Holy Spirit empowers us to say no to old desires that are sinful and say yes to the work of God in our lives, empowered by Him.

Therefore, brothers and sisters, we have an obligation—but it is not to the flesh, to live according to it. For if you live according to the flesh, you will die; but if by the Spirit you put to death the misdeeds of the body, you will live. (Romans 8:12–13)

Throughout Scripture, when the Spirit of God surfaces, there is power. We can claim this power to live for Jesus and do what is right whenever we need it.

I pray that out of his [God's] glorious riches he may strengthen you with power through his Spirit in your inner being. (Ephesians 3:16)

While the Holy Spirit can bring power, the power He brings is often in the daily emotions and interactions of our lives.

But the fruit of the Spirit is love, joy, peace, forbearance, kindness, goodness, faithfulness, gentleness and self-control. Against such things there is no law. (Galatians 5:22–23)

Conclusion

But we have this treasure in jars of clay to show that this all-surpassing power is from God and not from us.

2 Corinthians 4:7

On Jesus's final night with His disciples He did not give them a written quiz to test their mental recall of all He had taught them. The twelve men had been with Jesus for three years of lessons, miracles, teaching to thousands, and daily dialogue. Instead, Jesus grabbed a towel and began to wash the disciples' feet.

Almighty God used His human fingers to wipe manure, dust, and dirt from the toes of Judas, who would soon betray Him. He washed the arches, ankles, and heels of Peter, who would soon deny Him and fail Him in spectacular fashion.

As Jesus did this, He demonstrated the nature of God. He proved the theme of His entire ministry and incarnation on Planet Earth. Yes, precise beliefs connect a person to God, but that same God wants to capture our hearts and entire beings, not just our minds.

I subtitled this book "Christian Essentials for the Head *and the Heart*" because the Christian essentials grow cold and lifeless if we only think about them in our heads. Seminaries turn to cemeteries and churches turn to empty, cold buildings when Christ's followers fail to carry the good news in our hearts as well as our heads.

We must hold these truths in our hearts and let them affect all we are and all we do.

Now that you have confirmed your basic beliefs as true facts, let me encourage you to carry them in your heart. Invite the love and grace of God to become the mortar between every brick of "belief" you have established. Invite the Holy Spirit to inject His passion and compassion into the way you see yourself and every human being.

As you and I do this, we will see ourselves daily as God does: glorious yet imperfect, but ever being restored by Christ the Redeemer. We will see the evil people, the sinful, the addicts, and the dishonest politicians as Jesus sees them: with compassion. They, too, are glorious ruins in need of restoration. And we exist on earth to broadcast the good news of Christ to them.

Scripture warns us that "knowledge puffs up," and God says the solution to this is that "love builds up" (1 Corinthians 8:1). If we ever carry our biblical understanding as a weapon to harm others rather than a tool to free them from sin and slavery, then we have become "puffed up."

If we become more concerned with proving others wrong than with helping them be made right through Christ, then we have become "puffed up."

The solution is not to forsake knowledge. It is to elevate love. This is why Jesus, in His incarnation, came to humanity "full of grace and truth" (John 1:14). If we are to follow Him, we will be unflinchingly clear about the truth, even as we dirty our hands, bend on aching knees, and wash the feet of people who will betray us and fail us. "Grace and truth" intertwine intrinsically in the nature of our Messiah whom we follow and to whom the Holy Spirit empowers us to become more like each day.

In the opening text of this book, I mentioned how Christians and children are alike. Children grow by eating and exercising;

Christians grow by believing and obeying. This book focused largely on believing. But we cannot properly end this study of our basic beliefs without reminding ourselves that "belief" with Jesus always implies action—obedience. People act upon what they truly believe. So let us now go and live out what we have learned.

May we continue to grow in God's truth as we continue to read His Word and engage with Him in our minds. And may we always *obey*. May we do and practice what Jesus says—a life of actionable grace. Grace is not merely a feeling or good intention. Grace shows in dirty water running down our forearms as we serve those around us. May we become "full of grace and truth" as our Messiah is.

Full of truth, may we carry our unchanging beliefs with courage and confidence, clinging to them even if we are mocked or belittled.

And at the same time, may we live out the words that Jesus taught as the foot-washing water softened the skin of His hands before His crucifixion, while He washed 120 toes belonging to His imperfect disciples. As Jesus washed those toes He showed and declared the heart of God, and He said, "By this everyone will know that you are my disciples, if you love one another" (John 13:35).

Almighty God,

You have given us the gift of truth in Your living Word and in the Word who was made flesh. Please shape our hearts to be like Yours—full of grace and truth.

Please strengthen us to become more like You in our thinking, in our believing, and in our obeying. We desire to follow You with our hearts as well as our minds, with our lives as well as our souls.

We desire to become more like You in every interaction, Jesus. Help us carry the Light of the World. Help us know You more each day. Help us experience You. Help us reach those You have called us to reach. Help us train up those You have called us to train. Amen.

POSTSCRIPT

You did it. You've strengthened and clarified your grasp on the essential Christian beliefs. Now you can recall these basic beliefs anytime, anywhere, using the simple lyric, "Jesus loves me, this I know, for the Bible tells me so."

The same God who created light to shine into the darkness of the universe has now made His light shine in our hearts by giving us the light of the knowledge of Christ.

In an age of clanging noises and opinions, we can know with clarity these Christian essentials, which are nonnegotiable and which connect us into the light and power of God.

At the start of this book, I described these basic beliefs as the foundation of a house, and now you've confirmed the sturdy foundation of your faith in Christ. You've claimed what you believe. Way to go!

On this foundation you can now build so much more as you continue to believe what the Word of God says and obey Jesus. I encourage you to continue seeking God daily by reading His Word in *The Life Application Study Bible*, which I described earlier in this book.

I'd also be thrilled to encourage you daily. I text out a brief devotional video of Scriptural encouragement every day. You can begin receiving these messages by texting the word DAILY to 317-350-1996.

You can also connect with me on social media @JohnSDickerson.

If you'd like to get free study guides or learn about my other books, send an email to Friend@IAmStrongBook.com.

And finally, you can find small group videos and discussion questions for this book at JohnSDickerson.com.

Let's keep following our great God together.

Notes

Why Should You Read This Book?

1. Philippians 2:5–8.
2. 1 Peter 2:1–12.

What Is an Essential?

1. John 3:16–18.
2. Romans 12:1–2.
3. I am paraphrasing a story reported to me by some friends who read an early draft of this book. I cannot attest to this story's accuracy, but I have no reason to believe it is not true.

Death by School Bus

1. Most translations include "believe" and its variations seven times between John 3:12 and 18.
2. Proverbs 4:23.
3. Romans 12:1–2.

Chapter 2 The Messiah within the Trinity

1. Wayne Grudem, *Systematic Theology: An Introduction to Biblical Doctrine* (Grand Rapids: Zondervan, 2000), 231.
2. See John 3:16–18.

Chapter 4 Jesus Proves His Love with Actions

1. I wrote at length about the anxiety, pain, and suffering this produced in my book *I Am Strong: Finding God's Peace and Strength in Life's Darkest Moments*. If you want a free sample of that book, just send an email to Friend @IAmStrongBook.com.

Chapter 7 Glorious but Ruined

1. In a video at JohnSDickerson.com/media, I walk viewers through pictures of rusted junk. Each of those pictures looks like scrap metal. But each is actually a close-up of a classic "barn find" car that is a glorious ruin.
2. Hebrews 4:15.
3. See 2 Corinthians 5.
4. Philippians 1:6.
5. Philippians 1:6.

Chapter 8 Being Restored the Moment You Believe

1. See Titus 2:12.
2. See Galatians 5:1.
3. This is my paraphrase.
4. If you or someone you love is sick or living in a body that is falling apart, I encourage you to read or listen to my book *I Am Strong: Finding God's Peace and Strength in Life's Darkest Moments*. The audio is available on the Audible app, and the print book is available anywhere books are sold. *I Am Strong* details how we can continue choosing God, even as our bodies or emotions ache and flare with pain.
5. 1 Timothy 2:4.

Chapter 10 Knowing Your Salvation

1. Romans 5:8.
2. Colossians 2:14.
3. 1 John 2:2.
4. Matthew 19:24.

Chapter 11 Pictures of Your Salvation

1. I first told this same story, in more detail, in my book *I Am Strong*. This telling is a simplified reporting of the same documented events. In my years as a pastor and researcher, I have not found any better visual to demonstrate what Jesus did for us on the cross. I recommend *I Am Strong* for anyone who is facing sickness or discouragement.
2. Romans 5:12.
3. I am paraphrasing here not to put words in Jesus's mouth but rather to try to capture the essence of His many claims around this theme.
4. 1 Timothy 2:4.
5. I first told this story about Mickey in my book *The Great Evangelical Recession*. I recommend *The Great Evangelical Recession* for any ministry leaders, whether pastors and paid staff or volunteers. The book is designed to help boards, elders, deacons, and other leaders guide their ministries through the financial and cultural challenges that Christian ministries will face in the next decade.
6. See Romans 8, particularly the end of the chapter.

Chapter 13 Jesus's Standard for What You Believe

1. Hebrews 4:15.

2. For a more complete list of these brilliant Jesus followers who believed every Word of Scripture to be divinely inspired by God, see my book *Jesus Skeptic: A Journalist Explores the Credibility and Impact of Christianity* (Grand Rapids: Baker Books, 2019).

3. See Ephesians 2:10; 2 Timothy 3:16–17.

4. There are passages of Scripture that say exactly what to take off and what to put on (see Ephesians 5, Colossians 3, and 1 Peter 2).

Chapter 14 God's Love Letter to You

1. Psalm 1:3.

Chapter 16 The Holy Spirit

1. For the record, I deeply love this brother. Thank you, David and Julie, for paying for my first semester of seminary and being used by God to help me get a start in life. And, David, thank you also for popping up out of that water.

2. See Philippians 2.

3. See Matthew 3:16; Mark 1:10; Luke 3:22; John 1:32.

4. See Mark 1:12.

5. See Acts 10:38.

Chapter 17 The Power to Solve Your Greatest Problems

1. In my book *Jesus Skeptic*, I show the actual journals and writings of these and many other well-known heroes who were motivated by their faith in Christ. Evidence reveals that Jesus's followers played crucial roles in launching the Scientific Revolution, creating modern education, eradicating disease, ending open slavery, and so much more.

John S. Dickerson is a seminary-trained pastor and bestselling author. He serves as lead pastor of Connection Pointe Christian Church in Indiana and online at www.ConnectionPointe.org. A recognized voice in American Christianity, he has spoken at some of the most influential churches and seminaries in the country. His writing has appeared in the *New York Times* and *USA Today*, and he earned the Livingston Award for Young Journalists, given by Tom Brokaw of NBC News and Christiane Amanpour of CNN and ABC News. Learn more at JohnSDickerson.com.

Can we know if Jesus
actually lived?

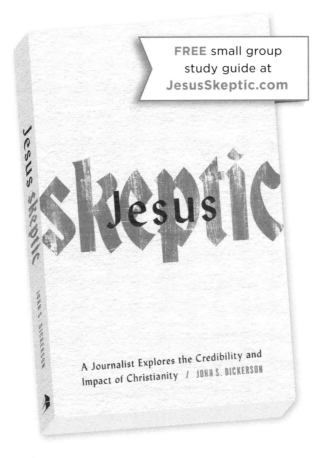

FREE small group
study guide at
JesusSkeptic.com

A first-of-its-kind book for a new generation, *Jesus Skeptic* takes
nothing for granted as it explores whether Jesus actually lived and
how his story has changed our world. In a generation that wants
to make the world a better place, we can discover what humanity's
greatest champions had in common: a Christian faith.

BakerBooks
a division of Baker Publishing Group
www.BakerBooks.com

Available wherever books and ebooks are sold.

Also Available from

JOHN S. DICKERSON

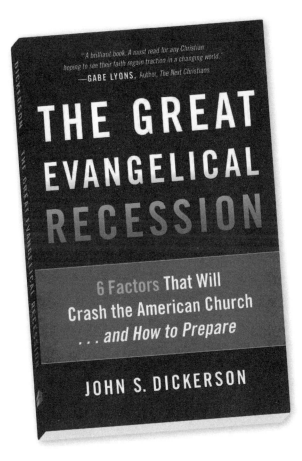

"A brilliant book. A must read for any Christian hoping to see their faith regain traction in a changing world."
—GABE LYONS, Author, The Next Christians

THE GREAT EVANGELICAL RECESSION

6 Factors That Will Crash the American Church
...and How to Prepare

JOHN S. DICKERSON

In *The Great Evangelical Recession*, award-winning journalist and pastor John S. Dickerson identifies six factors that are radically eroding the American church and offers biblical solutions to prepare us for spiritual success, even in the face of alarming trends.

To learn more about
John S. Dickerson's speaking and writing, visit

JOHNSDICKERSON.COM

   @JohnSDickerson